Living in the Retirement Zone

Alex Sutherland

LifePlan Group
RALEIGH, NORTH CAROLINA

Copyright © 2022 by Alex Sutherland.

All rights reserved. No part of this publication may be reproduced, distributed or transmitted in any form or by any means, including photocopying, recording, or other electronic or mechanical methods, without the prior written permission of the publisher, except in the case of brief quotations embodied in critical reviews and certain other noncommercial uses permitted by copyright law. For permission requests, write to the publisher at the address below.

We are a financial services firm helping our clients prepare for retirement through the use of insurance and investment products. LifePlan Group is a dba for LifePlan Investment Advisors, Inc., a Registered Investment Advisory firm registered with the U.S. Securities and Exchange Commission; and LifePlan Tax and Insurance Group, Inc., a firm licensed to sell insurance. We are not affiliated with any government agency, and do not offer tax or legal advice. Always consult with your own tax/legal advisors regarding your unique circumstances. This book is for informational purposes only and should not be construed as advice or a recommendation to purchase any product or employ any specific investment strategy. Investing involves risk, Including possible loss of principal. Insurance product guarantees are backed by the financial strength and claims-paying ability of the issuing company. Product and feature availability may vary by state.

Alex Sutherland/LifePlan Group
7201 Creedmoor Road #147
Raleigh, NC 27613
www.lifeplangroup.com

Book layout ©2013 BookDesignTemplates.com

Living in the Retirement Zone/Alex Sutherland, 1st ed.
ISBN 9798793208321

For my children,

Nora, Shea, and Elliot,

You inspire me every day to live life *in the zone*; may you discover your own zone and live it out – sooner rather than later!

Contents

Foreword i

Being in the 'Zone' 1

A Little About Us 11

'Unsuccessful' Money Habits 19

The Great Transition 35

What to Look for in an Advisor 49

Your Perfect Day 73

Retirement Realities and How to Address Them 81

Retirement Instruments: The Good and the Bad 99

Your Symphony: A True Financial Plan 121

The Retirement Zone 141

Foreword
By Ken Sutherland, CLU, ChFC

We all go through various transitions in life. Some of these we choose, while others are thrust upon us.

This book will help you navigate the most critical element in what we call the "Great Transition." "Great" refers to something that is big; "transition" is all about change.

Retirement is a very big change in your life. Typically, you are able to choose when this transition takes place; occasionally you are notified. Some will look forward to this for years, and others dread it, putting it off for as long as possible.

I mentioned above that "we" call this change in life the "Great Transition." When "we" are in the office, the author of this book refers to me as "Ken." However, away from the office, he calls me Dad. We are a father-and-son business. It is my pleasure and with pride that I write a foreword to this book that my son, Alex, has written. It is also with confidence that I recommend it to you, knowing it will help guide your transition into *Living in The Retirement Zone*.

Retirement is a big change in your life. This book is dedicated to not only making this transition good, but great!

Allow me to tell you a little about my own transition toward the Retirement Zone.

I love what I do. I get to help our clients best use their financial resources to live the life they wish to live, sooner rather than later. What's not to love about that? Twelve years ago, I wrote my vision for retirement using the same process that I, and now Alex, guide our clients through. Remember the movie, *Field of Dreams*? Remember the line, "Build it and they will come"? That was my approach to retirement planning. I wanted to retire at a lake house in warmer weather, living near our children, preferably passing my advisory firm onto one of them.

During the past decade, I moved my firm, LifePlan Group, from Nebraska to North Carolina, sparked by following all three of our children here. My wife and I are blessed to now live on a lake, near our children and six grandchildren (all arriving in the past seven years)! Several times a week, I'm on the lake slalom skiing by 6:30 a.m., followed by coffee on our deck and, oh, now and then going into the office to meet with clients.

Ten years ago, Alex mentioned he might enjoy joining me in this industry. "Awesome," I said. He could start a little below his teacher's salary sitting at the front desk answering the phones. This was a big career transition for him, and I wanted him to do it by choice and do it well. Over the years, he has sat at each desk in the office, mastering every skill necessary to run a successful advisory firm. Initially, he sat in on every client meeting I had, taking notes that we would later debrief. He learned a lot in this process, and guess what, so did I! Now, Alex runs our firm.

Along the way, I read Jim Collins' book, *Good to Great*, in which he asks the question, "Why do some businesses grow from being good to becoming great and are built to last?" His two primary discoveries point to leadership and getting the right people on the bus. I take some credit for building a good business that provided leadership, and I got Alex on the bus. He is now continuing to make this business great and built to last.

Alex and I are now asking you, "How will you make your retirement not just good but great, and built to last?"

The temptation you face is to dive into the details, crunch the numbers, evaluate optimal investment strategies all of which are necessary for a good retirement. Yet these details may very well derail a great retirement. Too many people put off life while trying to perfect strategies. Often the best savers fear spending, even though they have enough.

Enough for what? That's the critical retirement question. "What's it all about, Alfie?" (If you are anywhere near my age, you remember this 1967 Dionne Warwick song and its call to a deeper life!) What's the life you want to live, what's the true purpose of your money? Why not make this chapter of life your best chapter?

These are not touchy-feely questions. They are central to Living in the Retirement Zone. Addressing these questions will better determine all the details that follow.

I believe everyone facing or already living in retirement would do well to seek good leadership and get the right people on their bus. Find an advisor who will lead you through a rich discovery process that can help you focus on what's most important to you. They can then help you best use your financial resources to live the life you most wish to live, sooner rather than later.

What's not to love about that? Reading this book is a great place to start your Great Transition!

Ken Sutherland, CLU, ChFC
Master of Divinity Degree in Theology
(Alex's Dad)

CHAPTER ONE

Being in the 'Zone'

Have you ever been "in the zone"? Athletes talk about it, that rare moment in time when being at their very best seems almost effortless. For a basketball player, it might be the night when every shot they take swishes through the net. For a golfer, it could be the round when every 10-foot putt finds the bottom of the cup. For the distance runner, it could be that blissful period when the pain and exhaustion subsides, time no longer matters, and they just ... run.

Even the most elite performers can be surprised to find themselves in the zone. As a kid, I vividly remember watching the Chicago Bulls play the Portland Trailblazers in Game 1 of the 1992 NBA Finals. Michael Jordan, already known as one of basketball's all-time greats, was having an especially great game. Almost every shot he took was going in, even from three-point range. At one moment in the game, after draining yet another long-distance shot with apparent ease, Jordan jogged back to his end of the court, looked at the announcers who were calling the game, and just shrugged, as if to say, "I don't even know how I'm doing it." This iconic moment is captured on YouTube and in the excellent 2020 ESPN documentary about the Chicago Bulls teams of the 1990s, *The Last Dance*. To me, it's one of the most memorable, shining examples of someone being in the zone.

Like Jordan and his shrug, many other great competitors have expressed mysticism and awe about the zone. Legendary tennis player Billie Jean King once described it as a perfect combination of "violent action taking place in an atmosphere of total tranquility."

"When it happens," she said, "I want to stop the match and grab the microphone and shout, 'That's what it's all about!' Because it is. It's not the big prize I'm going to win at the end of the match, or anything else. It's just having done something that's totally pure and having experienced the perfect emotion."

The zone isn't limited to sports, of course. I remember my first experience with it many years ago, as lead trumpet for a big band while I was a high school senior in Omaha.

One particular week, I'd been having a tough time with my part for an upcoming concert. One song, called "My Lament" by the composer Maria Schneider, was giving me particular trouble. My band director suggested that I hand my part off to the backup trumpet player, and I responded by saying, "no way."

The night of the performance at the University of Nebraska at Omaha, I took the stage feeling incredibly focused and poised. Playing as part of a big band is a powerful, soul-stirring experience, but there was something even more special about this particular concert. I simply played the best I had ever played — I was calm, I was at ease, and I was living entirely in the present. Time seemed to slow down, while at the same time, it flashed by in a blur.

I can't explain the moment — which I hadn't experienced as a trumpeter — other than to simply say that I was in the zone.

My big band days are long past me, but I haven't stopped thinking about the zone and how it can be applied to other aspects of life. You don't have to be an athlete or an artist or a musician to experience it.

As a financial advisor, I truly believe that there is such a thing as a "Retirement Zone" — it means spending your time doing what gives you the most joy, fulfillment, and pleasure during your retirement years. We've all watched people bask in the awe and ecstasy of the zone, and I believe those who are planning and preparing for retirement can experience this as well.

It all comes down to how you choose to live your life, and how you plan to spend time doing the things you love the best. Identifying what you treasure most about life — and how to enjoy it now — is the first step to building a financial plan that will give you the freedom and resources to do all those things that are the most meaningful during retirement.

Then, you'll truly be in the zone.

Putting the money to work

When you seek out a financial advisor to help you plan for your retirement, your focus is likely on the financial picture. What investment vehicles, what products, and what tax strategies will ensure a financially successful retirement?

These are important considerations, of course, but your first questions should be about what you actually want to *do* during retirement and who you want to *be*. How do you envision it? What, to you, would be an enjoyable and successful retirement? What brings you contentment, joy, and fulfillment? And, finally, *when* do you want to make this transition? Once you tackle those questions, then a strategy can be formed to achieve those goals. Money is important, but, ultimately, it's a tool. Once you know what your retirement should look like and the financial cost to achieve that, then you can align that money to meet your goals.

Envisioning your retirement seems simple, but it's something many people struggle to do. Often, some of the most successful, career-oriented people have the hardest time articulating what the next stage of their lives should be like. Their identities are so intertwined with their working lives, they can't picture a time in life when that work is no longer necessary.

When I meet with new clients, there are two common concerns I hear again and again. One is the fear of running out of money and not having enough of it at the end of life.

It's a very valid concern, but one that can result in obsessively saving and putting off retirement indefinitely. Even if we rationally know we won't run out of money, we still often fear emotionally that we might.

The other concern is being eighty or eighty-five years old and saying, "I should have gone on more trips," or "I should have visited my grandkids more often." That is a fear of not using your money and not fully enjoying retirement when one has the ability to do so.

My role as an advisor is to help craft a plan that addresses and helps ease both of those concerns. I call it, "Walking the Retirement Tightrope." It's my job to help clients find that balance, that sweet spot between retiring too early and having a constant worry of money dwindling — or retiring too late and not getting to use the money living the life they most wish to live.

Two very different retirements

Anyone familiar with LifePlan Group has probably heard about Boots Sutherland. She's my grandmother and, on her seventy-fifth birthday, she took the unusual step of skydiving for the first time. "I'm really living now," she quipped after making her jump, which we captured on a video that we feature on the LifePlan homepage.

Boots traveled a lot during her retirement, including visits to Egypt to see the pyramids and to Scotland to trace her husband's family ancestry. Through all her days, she embodied living her best life, and her retirement was no exception. She was determined to make the most of it.

Her beloved husband of over fifty years, my Grandpa Al, was different. He was a World War II vet, kindhearted but also frugal; a Scotsman who saved well, but had difficulty enjoying his resources in retirement. He did not accompany Boots on her overseas trips, not even to his parents' homeland. Spending money traveling the world just wasn't Al's thing. Toward the end of his life, however, he seemed to regret it. "I wish I had taken more of those trips with your mother," was one of the last things he told my dad before he passed away.

My grandparents had a long, happy marriage. But they were two different people who had different approaches to retirement. Grandma Boots envisioned retirement as a time for her to do all the exciting things she had always wanted to do, but didn't have time for, when she was a full-time mother and a nurse. Grandpa Al was more of a home body.

He loved tinkering on projects around the house. It wasn't as natural for him to plan and go on big trips. Neither retirement style is right or wrong, but life goes fast, health changes, doing what you most want while you can is a great gift to give yourself and those you love. Ultimately, he might have wished he had gotten a little more out of that period of his life.

Getting into the Retirement Zone

As you can probably guess from the title, this book is about helping you to imagine, plan for and live your best possible retirement. It doesn't matter if your goal for retirement is to travel the world, write your memoirs, take up a new hobby, volunteer for a favorite charity, spend time with the grandkids or perfect your golf game. The point is to articulate the retirement life that works for *you*, then come up with a plan to achieve it.

Here are some of the key things this book will cover in the next few chapters:

1. How some of the money-saving habits you've learned and adopted during your working years aren't always helpful during your retirement.

2. How to prepare for and address some of the financial realities of retirement, like Social Security taxes and required minimum distributions.
3. Why it's important to find an advisor who understands your goals and your full financial picture, and can truly serve as an advisor, guiding you in financial decisions and strategies that work best for you.
4. How retirement can be a great transition, both financially and emotionally, and how developing the right mindset can be as important as having the right financial resources.

I think for many of us, our money can be a little abstract while we are working. It's almost like Monopoly money. You see the retirement savings statements come in the mail and you check your 401(k) balance online, but it doesn't really mean anything tangible. It's a number on a page.

When you get to retirement, however, that money becomes very real. What does that money mean to you, and what can it do for you? Throughout this book, I'll share exercises to help you answer that question, as well as best practices about the specifics of money, investing and tax strategies.

Ultimately, as a result of reading this book, I hope you will better understand your resources, gain clarity on the ability they provide to help you live out the life you most wish to live, and have building blocks in place for a great financial plan.

Whether you are currently retired or are thinking about it in the near future, I hope this book will set you on the path to addressing both those concerns I described: the fear of running out of money and the fear of not living retirement to the fullest.

When retirement is done right, I've had clients describe it to me as the best stage of their lives. That certainly can be true for you, as well.

So, what do you say? Are you ready to get into the Retirement Zone? Let's get started.

CHAPTER TWO

A Little About Us

Our advisory firm, LifePlan Group, is a family business. My father, Ken Sutherland, formed it over two decades ago, and I joined LifePlan in 2012. As founder and investment advisor, my dad remains our visionary leader and continues to serve his clients, some of whom have been with him from the very beginning. As LifePlan's president, I am also an investment advisor, in addition to directing our company's day-to-day operations.

I know you didn't pick up this book to read a long, rambling story about the Sutherland family history. Most of us don't particularly care to read much about other people unless those other people are famous.

However, I did want to share a little about our backgrounds to help you understand how LifePlan came about, and what makes our firm unique in the way we serve our clients. I promise to keep it brief!

Before he started a career in financial services, my father was a Lutheran minister.

My dad loved the ministry and his congregation at Holy Cross Lutheran Church in Salem, Oregon. But as the father of three young children, he wasn't so fond of the fact that much of his work as a minister took place on the weekends. As a pastor, he found it challenging to spend time with his young, growing family at times when they were free. His pastoral work seemed to be getting in the way of becoming the person and the father that he wanted to be.

So my dad made one of his most difficult decisions and switched careers. He worked in insurance, charitable giving, and tax planning for a few years before founding his own financial firm, LifePlan Group, in 1995. Being an advisor was work that he found fulfilling, and that still allowed him to serve others and be a part of their lives. He also got his weekends back — for the most part.

In fact, my dad discovered soon after starting his own business that he often learned more personal details about his clients as an advisor than he ever did as a minister for his congregants. In a way, I think that speaks volumes to the closeness people can feel for their financial advisor, and the important roles those advisors can play.

Growing up, I always knew that someday I would like to be a part of my father's business. In fact, I wanted to be just like him — as a small child, I used to bring my kid-sized briefcase to the LifePlan office, and Dad and I would "work" together.

However, despite my desire to join the family firm, my father and I agreed it would be best to gain some outside world experience first. He once told me, "You need to join this industry because you want to join this industry. Not because your father is in it."

So I carved my own path, graduating with a double-major in engineering and music from Iowa State. As I entered the job market, I quickly realized that for me personally, the mostly introverted, computer-based work of being an entry-level employee at an engineering firm was not going to satisfy my creative energy or my desire to be around and collaborate with other people.

Right out of the gate, I took a career detour, signing up with an organization called Teach for America, which trains people who don't have backgrounds in education to teach students in underserved parts of the country. After an extensive summer training through Teach for America, I became a high school math teacher in Warren County, North Carolina.

For two years, my job was to teach high school students to love math, specifically Algebra II and precalculus. That wasn't an easy task, by any means, but I loved the work, and I ended up being a pretty good teacher. During a summer school stint in Tulsa, Oklahoma, I was given five weeks to show students that math, rather than being a boring, complicated chore, could be a creative, even exciting experience. Teach for America documented my assignment in a video, in which students described their perceptions about math at the beginning of summer school, and how those perceptions changed near the end of the summer.

"I can actually go into a test feeling confident and feeling that I'm going to pass, other than being scared, biting my nails, all that stuff," one student said. "Since fourth grade, this is the first time I've actually had an 'A' in math."

Those two years of high school teaching combined three things that give me joy: (1) working with people, (2) being creative, and (3) working with math and numbers. I interacted with students and their parents, I prepared lesson plans and I got to share my passion for mathematics.

When my stint in Warren County concluded, I made the decision to walk away from teaching. Given that my mother was a career third-grade teacher, and I had always held teachers in the highest regard, this was a very emotional, difficult decision. While I loved working with students, I just couldn't envision the life I wanted to build through my teaching career.

It was 2012, and I decided to become an investment advisor. Fortunately, I knew a pretty good mentor just about an hour's drive away in Raleigh. My father had moved LifePlan to North Carolina a few years earlier, so that he and my mom could live on a lake that was also close to me, my older brother and my younger sister, who all lived in the Tar Heel State by that time.

Initially, I didn't become an advisor at LifePlan right away. I started out by answering the phones, shadowing my father, getting my licenses, and learning the business. Ten years in, I now run the firm, while Dad continues to serve his clients in his transition toward retirement.

Like teaching, LifePlan allows me to do the three things I love: work with people, be creative and work with math. Though my teaching career was relatively short, I have to say that I wouldn't be the advisor I am today without that experience.

Serving our clients is my version of sustainable teaching. At LifePlan, we put a lot of time and effort into ensuring our clients fully understand the plans we've crafted for their retirement, not just through one-on-one meetings, but through monthly events like our Lunch & Learns and our late afternoon Wine & Wisdoms, as well as yearly get-togethers like our LifePlan Summit, State of the Economy, and our annual picnic. The topics of these sessions aren't just limited to investing, tax strategy, and financial products — we bring guest speakers ranging from economists to Research Triangle professors to talk about what's happening in the U.S. economy and the world at large.

I suspect most advisory firms don't provide their clients with an annual calendar of events specifically planned for them. At LifePlan, we do it in our effort to be educational, to give back to our community, and to be a meaningful part of our clients' lives. It's what we call "Investing in Your Life," meaning that your money can do a lot more than just sit in a retirement account and grow. It has a job to do in helping you live your best life. At LifePlan, we try to exemplify that ethos by directing some of our resources toward speakers and events that we believe will bring value to our clients and our community.

As a former pastor, my dad found a different way to experience fellowship and to serve others as an investment advisor with his own independent firm. As a former teacher, I have found that what gives me the most satisfaction as an advisor is when a client "gets it." They make that connection between the financial resources they have and the retirement they want to live, and a plan to make that happen starts coming together. It's not too different from those moments I experienced as a teacher when my high school students learned to appreciate and even enjoy Algebra II or precalculus.

That's why, no matter how much our organization grows, we will always be focused on working personally with our clients.

After all, it's a combination of the three things that give me the most joy.

CHAPTER THREE

'Unsuccessful' Money Habits

In the world of business, you'd be hard-pressed to find someone who is more respected and admired than Warren Buffett. For decades, the "Oracle of Omaha" and his diversified holding company, Berkshire Hathaway, have been upheld as the standard-bearers for successful, long-term investment strategies. As of December 2020, Buffett's net worth was estimated to be over $85 billion, making him the fourth-wealthiest person in the world.

Despite his enormous wealth, Buffett is nearly as famous for his relatively frugal lifestyle. His home in Omaha is in a nice neighborhood, but it's modest for someone in his income bracket. A noted philanthropist, Buffett has pledged to give 99 percent of his fortune to charitable causes, much of it through the Bill & Melinda Gates Foundation.

In short, Buffett seems to value steady, methodical growth for his wealth instead of spending it. "Our favorite holding period is forever," is just one of Buffett's many famous quotes about money and investing.

All of which is extremely laudable — but not all of us are the Oracle of Omaha. In fact, none of us are.

And many of us would prefer to *spend* some of the wealth we have accumulated while we are still living.

However, that's not so easy to do, especially if you've spent your working years carefully, methodically and responsibly saving for your retirement. Those good habits you've cultivated during the pre-retirement years of accumulating wealth — saving money, living below your means, investing properly — don't translate very well to the distribution phase of your life. In fact, those habits can be detrimental.

When I first got into this industry, I used to think that the clients who had the greatest amounts of money would have the easiest time retiring, but I soon learned that it often was exactly the opposite. Those who saved very well for retirement usually had the most difficulty retiring, and shifting their focus from the challenge of building wealth to the new challenge of spending it.

It's an interesting dynamic, and one I never could have predicted as I started my career as an advisor. In this chapter, we'll examine why frugality isn't always a virtue during retirement, and I'll share some steps you can take to change your mindset from that of a dedicated saver to a practical spender.

The origin of 'living beneath your means'

The baby boomers have been written about and documented more than perhaps any other American generation. But did you know that many boomers tend to be excellent savers?

Recent data bears this out. The average American baby boomer household (between the ages of fifty-two and seventy) has a net worth of $1.2 million.[1] According to a

---

[1] Mallika Mitra. Aug. 8, 2019. CNBC. "Baby boomers' wealth is 12 times greater compared to millennials. Here's why."
https://www.cnbc.com/2019/08/08/baby-boomers-wealth-is-12-times-greater-compared-to-millennials.html

recent report by the TransAmerica Center for Retirement Studies, only 4 percent of boomers say they have taken an early withdrawal from a 401(k) or a similar plan — compared with 10 percent of Generation Xers and 15 percent of millennials.[2]

It's not all rosy for the boomers, though. A 2019 report by the Insured Retirement Institute found that a shocking 45 percent of those baby boomers surveyed had no retirement savings at all.[3] For the other 55 percent, however, saving has been a part of their DNA, likely influenced by parents and grandparents who suffered through the Great Depression.

The Depression of the 1930s, as you likely know, had a devastating impact on millions of American lives. At one point, nearly a third of the country was unemployed. Bank failures meant that many American families lost their life savings.

While the Depression did finally end, it left a lingering effect on the American psyche. For many people, frugality

---

[2] Martha C. White. July 2, 2021. The New York Times. "A Struggle for the Millennials." https://www.nytimes.com/2021/07/02/business/retirement-millennials-personal-finance.html

[3] Insured Retirement Institute. 2019. "Boomer Expectations for Retirement 2019." https://www.myirionline.org/docs/default-source/default-document-library/iri_babyboomers_whitepaper_2019_final.pdf?sfvrsn=55bc4364_0

became a way of life. Saving was a virtue, whether it was money, food, or other resources. Have you ever known an older relative who refused to throw away a sheet of used tinfoil because that would be "wasteful"? That mentality likely emerged from a personal experience in the Great Depression.

Many baby boomers grew up in homes where not being wasteful and saving for a rainy day were the norms. Those habits were passed down to millions of boomers who, despite the ever-growing societal pressure of living in a material world, learned to live beneath their means. In other words, they made a practice of spending less than their incomes brought in. Instead of living paycheck to paycheck, or taking on unwieldy debt, they had money left over each month to put into savings, invest in the stock market or sock away into a 401(k) or an individual retirement account.

Now, many of those people are in their late fifties or sixties and transitioning into retirement. Perhaps you're one of them. Over the years, you've diligently saved or invested a portion of your income, and watched with some satisfaction as your well-balanced and diversified portfolio has steadily gained in value. You may have even read some of the bestsellers out there, like *Rich Dad, Poor Dad* or *The*

Millionaire Next Door, books that encourage thrifty living and building wealth. You've taken the time to learn how money works, how the government and the American economy work, and you've been determined to *make your money work for you* through reinvested dividends and careful portfolio management.

I used to think that the wealthiest people in life were the ones who lived in the fanciest McMansion or drove the flashiest imported sports cars. But that's often not the case. Many of those people who live the flashy lifestyle are spending beyond their means and swimming in debt. They are the pleasure-seeking grasshoppers when compared with the industrious ants, the people who have *real* wealth, but often live in modest homes, drive practical vehicles, and benefit from the power of compound interest. They don't show off their wealth, or get caught up in the "keeping up with the Joneses" mentality. Like Buffett, their favorite holding period may be forever.

The New York Times published a story about Sylvia Bloom, a legal secretary from Brooklyn who amassed a fortune, then donated $8.2 million to charity upon her death. How did she accumulate such wealth? Simple: she lived a frugal life, made smart investments, worked for the same law firm for sixty-seven years before retiring at age ninety-six, and died not long afterward in 2016.

Bloom's niece and the executor of her estate told *The Times* she had no idea of her aunt's wealth until after she died. "I (then) realized she had millions," said the niece, "and she had never mentioned a word. I don't think she thought it was anybody's business but her own."

Most of us lack the dedication and discipline of a Sylvia Bloom, but the clients I see are generally good savers, typically building a household net worth in the seven figures by the time they approach retirement. Generally, they are self-made people, and not the beneficiaries of a big inheritance. They understand the value of hard work, earning money and maxing out their 401(k)s and IRA contributions.

You might be like them. You've run the race, worked very hard and made careful, calculated moves in saving your money for retirement.

Now, you're about to make that transition, and it's time to move from a savings mindset to one of spending.

How, exactly, do you do that?

Are you a saver or a spender?

One easy exercise you can do to find out how comfortable you'll be with the distribution phase of retirement is to ask yourself a simple question: "Am I a saver, or am I a spender?"

If you can't readily answer that question, think back to the last time you received an unexpected lump sum of money. Maybe it was a surprisingly large year-end bonus, a tax refund, or even a government stimulus check during the COVID-19 pandemic.

What was your immediate reaction to that money? Was it to spend it, or to save it? How you naturally reacted to that little windfall should put you clearly into one camp or another. Natural spenders have a challenge in saving and preparing for retirement. If you're in the "saver" camp (and chances are good, if you're reading this book, that you are a saver), you're likely to be better positioned for retirement. Giving yourself permission to spend during retirement is going to be the hard part for you.

Some of my clients do not want to continue amassing wealth in their later years like a Warren Buffet or a Sylvia Bloom. They might not be motivated to leave as large of an estate as possible at the end of their lives. Often, they tell me, "I want to use my money when I retire on the things I love. I want to travel; I want to give back to charity; I want to spend time with my grandkids."

As an advisor, however, a big part of my job is to help clients give themselves permission, again and again, to spend their money. They want to enjoy their retirement life but also have a mental roadblock on spending their life savings.

Spending assets is different from spending income. When you have a job, you know that income will continue to flow even as you spend it. When you no longer have a paycheck, and you're drawing from your life savings to spend it, that money goes away. You're "dipping into" a mountain of wealth you worked so hard to build.

Let me give you a specific example. If you are collecting Social Security benefits (and if not yet, imagine that you are), how difficult is it to spend that income? Probably pretty easy! Just live another thirty days and get another check. But what about spending that same amount of money from your 401(k) or IRA account — not as easy, is it? It is common to have a mental block in how we feel between spending income and spending assets. (By the way, Social Security is an asset. You paid into it your entire working career. The Social Security Administration just doesn't share with you the value of that asset, just the monthly income!)

A common question I encounter when encouraging my clients to take on more of a "spender" mentality is, "Will I have enough?"

I choose to answer that with a follow-up question: "Enough for what?"

In determining how much money is enough, we must understand and know what we want to do in life. Anything that is saved beyond meeting those goals is extra, unless we want to leave a significant inheritance. This is the fundamental building block to a great financial plan. At LifePlan, we call this the "Alpha" dollars, or "A" dollars for short. It's the amount of money it takes on a monthly or annual basis to pay the bills and enjoy life. If you don't know your "A" dollars, in a moment, I'll help you figure out what it actually is. It is important to know that all great components of a financial plan start with this figure. We believe it to be the most important when designing a financial plan.

So, once we know what we want to do as we transition into retirement, how do we reach a comfort level that we have "enough," and are able to give ourselves permission to spend?

There's a formula that might help.

How much is enough?

How do we turn our assets into income that we feel comfortable spending?

There's more than one way to do it. Often, it takes a different investment approach than the one you use when you're working. When you're working, you want to position your assets to grow.

The classic example is buying stock. Stocks are good at growing in the long term. They're not as good at maintaining stability. Imagine wanting to generate dependable income based on the month-to-month value of a stock. It would likely be pretty volatile — lots of ups and downs. We'll talk more about strategic shifts in managing your assets later in the book.

Regarding the investment strategy you use, my recommendation is to always find one that is effective for your specific needs and makes you feel comfortable. One pitfall that people sometimes run into is using a general guideline and applying it to their very specific situation. This approach is similar to taking medication to treat symptoms, but never visiting a doctor. The doctor is valuable, of course, because he or she can provide a care plan that works specifically for you.

One common guideline is the so-called Four Percent Rule — the theory made popular in the 1990s that, if you draw 4 percent of your retirement savings on an annual basis (for example, $40,000 each year from a $1 million portfolio), you won't run out of money in retirement. The idea being that the dividends and interest you accumulate each year will make up for that 4 percent you withdraw. Financial experts are split on whether the Four Percent Rule is still a safe approach in our current low interest rate environment. Personally, I view this rule to be outdated in today's world, and I'm always wary of a "one size fits all" approach to something as complex and important as retirement savings.

To establish if you have enough money to live in your Retirement Zone, you'll need to determine two things:

1. The cost of your desired lifestyle. (What we call "A" dollars)

2. If your savings, appropriately invested, is sufficient to support that desired lifestyle.

We're going to discuss your retirement lifestyle more later on so if you are having a difficult time coming up with a number of how much you'll need to spend each year — that's okay. Let me give you a quick easy way to get started on determining your "A" dollars. Typically for clients, their lifestyle cost doesn't dramatically change the day before retirement to the day after. One easy approach is just determining what you are currently spending and using that number. Get the last twelve months of bank statements and add up all of the outflows — the expenses. This will give you a good idea for a starting number to use. (One side comment: If you prefer to think in terms of monthly — just divide that number by 12. I usually suggest clients think of this number in whichever way makes most sense to them, typically, either as an annual figure, or monthly figure.)

Once you've arrived at that number, you'll want to calculate how much money you have relative to how much you are planning to spend. Here's a four-step way to do that:

1. List all your savings and investment accounts. Total them up and write down that number.

2. Write down your desired income that you will spend on an annual basis in your retirement. This is your "A" dollars that you just determined.
3. Subtract from that desired income what you expect to receive from Social Security and a pension (if you have one). The number you arrive at is called your "gap."
4. Divide that gap amount from your total financial account assets from step 1.

If the percentage you calculate is less than 3 percent, you're likely in good shape. If it's greater than 3 percent, but less than 5 percent, you're in the grey area. If you're greater than 5 percent, then there's a concern.

Here's a fictional, but real life-sounding example of the formula. Stan and Kathy are preparing to retire after more than four decades of working, saving, and living a comfortable, but not-too-flashy lifestyle. Over time, they've carefully built up a healthy portfolio of $2 million in income-producing assets.

Stan and Kathy estimate they'll need annual spending of $100,000 to live comfortably, do some traveling, and pursue other interests. From that $100,000, they subtract the

$60,000 they'll receive each year from Social Security and Stan's government pension. Therefore, their income gap is $40,000.

When dividing $40,000 from their $2 million in savings, Stan and Kathy arrive at 2 percent, which is very good news! That percentage indicates they should be able to comfortably live within their means during retirement — provided that they stick to their annual $100,000 spending estimate.

Using the same formula, another fictional couple, Greg and Linda, want to know if they can comfortably retire while also spending $100,000 a year. Their retirement savings total $1.2 million, and they'll receive $40,000 annually from Social Security. So, the gap between their income-producing assets and Social Security is $60,000. When dividing that number against their $1.2 million in assets, Greg and Linda come up with 5 percent — which means they'll want to build their nest egg up a little bit more if they expect to retire on $100,000 a year.

Again, everyone's situation is unique, but the four-step approach I just outlined is a fairly simple way to calculate how much money is enough for your retirement, and whether it will sustain you for the rest of your life.

The tricky part is that your finances and retirement are not static — they are likely to change over time. Also, what if you want to spend more money early in your retirement, rather than later on? The numbers move, which makes this type of planning very challenging and often needs dedicated planning software, we call ours the LifePlan Map™, but the four-step model is a good starting point in providing a snapshot of how you are doing in meeting your retirement goals.

It won't work, however, until you identify what retirement will look like for you, and how much that retirement is going to cost. In the next chapter, we'll examine what I call the Great Transition from working life to retirement.

What will that transition look like for you? Will you go from working full-time one week to lounging on the beach the next? More and more often, older adults are choosing a more gradual shift from their careers into retirement, a trend that is likely to grow even stronger in light of how the pandemic has changed the workplace for many Americans over the past two years.

What will your Great Transition possibly be? Read on for a few ideas, and a real-life example.

CHAPTER FOUR

The Great Transition

I was just beginning to think and write about the transition from a person's career to their retirement when the news scrolled across the bottom of my TV screen. It was big news — especially in the state of North Carolina.

Roy Williams announced his retirement after eighteen seasons as the head basketball coach at the University of North Carolina, and forty-four years in college coaching overall.

You may remember his farewell press conference on April 1, 2021. Ol' Roy was a coaching personality whose emotions always bubbled close to the surface. He was known to sometimes cry in the locker room after a tough loss, especially if it happened earlier than expected in the NCAA tournament. So, in his final press conference as UNC's coach, Roy Williams was characteristically blunt, raw, and painfully emotional.

His stated reason for retiring: "I no longer think I am the right man for the job."

In the world of sports, it's not unusual for a successful, beloved coach to hang on a little too long, then ultimately make a sad departure. "I just can't coach 'em anymore," was something that legendary college football coach Paul "Bear" Bryant said shortly before retiring from Alabama in 1982. Less than a month later, he passed away.

Even if you aren't a Tar Heel fan, he deserves credit for recognizing that the college game was changing, and that he no longer had the passion to change his coaching style along with it. At age seventy, he felt it was time to turn the page to a new chapter in life.

But in that press conference, Williams also seemed burned out. The abruptness and emotion of his retirement left me wondering how much planning and preparation he had made for this moment. Would he ease into an administrative position at UNC, take on a broadcasting gig for ESPN (as many former coaches do), or would he move on to a quieter, less-active life? "I'm scared to death of the next phase," Williams admitted at the time.

My point in reflecting on Roy Williams is not because it was such a public example of a high-profile coach retiring. It's that the move from working life to retirement can be a complex, challenging, hard-to-navigate process.

At LifePlan, we call this period the Great Transition. Ideally, you want to have a plan in place for how you are going to transition from working to retirement. You don't necessarily want to work until you decide, "I just can't do this anymore," and then turn in your two weeks' notice.

These days, the old cliché of a retirement party and a gold watch for the loyal associate who put in thirty-plus years of hard work at the old firm is becoming a rarity. Workers are more mobile than ever before. The Bureau of Labor Statistics reported that the average person would have *twelve jobs* between the ages of eighteen and fifty.[4] That number would likely be much higher if the age range expanded to sixty or sixty-five.

---

[4] Bureau of Labor Statistics. Aug. 31, 2021. "Number of Jobs, Labor Market Experience, Marital Status, and Health: Results from a National Longitudinal Survey." https://www.bls.gov/news.release/pdf/nlsoy.pdf

At the same time, many employers are less loyal to older workers, who are, in my opinion, often unfairly perceived as too expensive and too slow to adapt to new technology. Experience can sometimes be seen as a hindrance instead of an advantage. Because of ageism in the marketplace, finding a new job in your field after age fifty can be daunting. Therefore, many workers opt for an "encore career," moving into other disciplines like teaching, consulting, nonprofit work, or a passion project to bridge the gap between their fifties and the age at which they hope to retire. Some people voluntarily opt for an encore career — they're tired of what they've been doing, but they still want to keep working, and continue providing value to others.

Staging this kind of transition — as opposed to continuing to do what you've been doing until you are let go or get burned out — requires a bit of personal reflection and planning.

When thinking about the encore career, I'm reminded of a client who had enjoyed a very successful career in corporate sales. The problem was, my client was in his late fifties, still a few years away from when he wanted to fully retire, but wanted to walk away from the pressure and stress of his sales position. We worked with him to determine how much he yet needed to earn and then to identify an encore career — something less stressful (and less lucrative) than sales, but a career to pursue until he wanted to fully step away from the workforce.

Today, my client teaches history at a local community college and couldn't be happier. He's making less money than he would be as a sales executive, but he's more relaxed, more fulfilled, and the encore career fits nicely into his family's retirement plan.

Even if you don't have an encore career, to successfully make your Great Transition, you'll also want to know what retirement track you're currently on, and when you'll be able to transition your way to true financial freedom.

Illustrating your transition

When we talk to our clients about the Great Transition, we often show them a simple chart with a vertical line down the middle. On the left side of the line is a stage called "Working," and on the right side is one called "Retirement."

The line represents the Great Transition, which is a big event. It can be exciting. It can be nerve-wracking. It can also be empowering or daunting. It's a change. So, when we think about your money on the left side of the transition, while you're working, if I were to ask you, "What's the primary purpose of your money while you're working?" you would probably answer, "I want it to grow."

The other side of the transition, "Retirement," is the trickier part. In that stage, we provide three lines that illustrate the outcome of your money from retirement to the end of life. Line 1 is a scenario in which the money keeps growing, even as you take distributions. On Line 2, your money diminishes during the course of retirement, but there are still funds left over at the time of death. Line 3 represents a situation in which your money runs out before *you* run out — definitely a scenario that no retiree wants to experience.

Working
Accumulating Wealth

Retirement
Distributing Wealth

Line 1

Line 2

Line 3

$

We share this chart with clients to determine what line in retirement they are currently on or think they are on, and what line they'd like to be on. With Line 1, the result leaves a sizable estate upon death. However, not everybody wants to do that. Many people want to spend and enjoy their money during retirement, and hopefully leave some money to their beneficiaries. They want to be Line 2. But herein lies the challenge of the "saver." We emotionally want Line 1. It feels right for our money to grow — "savers" are used to that, but rationally we don't want to leave a big estate!

The point of this exercise is to help you understand, once you do retire, what the primary purpose of your money is. What words would you use to describe it? Clients often share with me words like income, security, or safety. All of these are different words than "grow." They can result in a different purpose for your money and how you allocate it for the future.

One of the things you have to ask yourself is, if you aren't yet retired: How much money do you need to have in order to retire?

Once we address these variables and determine which of the three lines most align with your goals — hopefully, Line 1 or Line 2 — we can then arrive at what we call Freedom Day, that glorious and profound moment when you are in a position to be financially free and independent, while no longer having to work to support the lifestyle and income that you want.

Freedom Day means having the freedom to safely do whatever you want. For some of us — and maybe even you — that means the freedom to *continue to work*. But that work might take on a bit of a different form.

Take my father, for example.

Waterskiing, bark mulch, and work

When my father, Ken Sutherland, crafted a vision statement for LifePlan Group in 2008, his hope was that, ultimately, one of his children would take over the business, or that he would be able to position LifePlan to be sold.

Unlike some entrepreneurs, my dad never planned to run the business until he physically or emotionally couldn't. He could see a day coming when he would want to have a succession plan, an exit plan, or both.

Today, that succession plan is in place. I lead the day-to-day operations at LifePlan. However, my father remains our visionary leader, my trusted mentor, and an advisor to his existing clients. He's still involved in the business, but not at the same level he was a few years ago.

This is my father's version of the Great Transition. He is 66 today, and the plan is to continue serving his clients for a few more years. Some of those clients go all the way back to when he first started our firm. They're more like friends, and almost like family. When one of them passes away, my Dad is often the first or second person that the surviving spouse calls.

But being there for his clients doesn't require a full-time commitment to LifePlan anymore. Dad typically works the first two weeks of each month, on Tuesday, Wednesday, and Thursday. Some months, he takes off of work entirely.

The miracle of modern technology enables him to work remotely much of the time, from his lake home in rural North Carolina that is about forty minutes from the nearest Target store. When he's not working, Dad enjoys a range of outdoor activities that include waterskiing and landscaping around his house. He and my mom are training their dog to be a therapy dog. Like most grandparents, they love that they're now able to spend more time with their grandkids.

So my dad's still working, but it's not the focal point of his life, the way it was for so many years. For him, the "aha" moment came a few years ago, when he realized that he had the financial flexibility to continue doing what he liked most about being an advisor (i.e., working with his clients), but he could hand off the administrative and business development duties at LifePlan that he no longer wanted to do. Today, I oversee that work.

Another key to my dad's Great Transition was figuring out what things he wanted to do on a typical day of retirement — things like enjoying the lake or working in the yard. He is now "in the zone" when he is slalom skiing at 6:30 in the morning! The other day, he admitted to being a few minutes late for a call with me because his was picking up bark mulch for the garden beds — the yard needed to look just right for Easter Sunday and a visit from the grandchildren. His mind was on other things besides business, and that's okay.

"One of the things I have always asked my clients who are preparing to retire is, 'What are the things you really want to do in life?'" Dad says. "In other words, when you're not traveling and doing some of the big-ticket things you want to do during retirement, what do you want to do with your downtime, when you're just at home? What is it like for you to be present, to know what you want life to be about now. When you get a sense of that, it's empowering, and that's freedom."

Five questions

In 2016, Harvard Dean James Ryan got up to deliver a commencement speech to the graduating class of the university's Graduate School of Education. What he said to them that afternoon quickly went viral on YouTube, and eventually led to a bestselling book.

Dean Ryan posed to the class "five truly essential questions that you should regularly ask yourself and others." While those questions were intended for graduate students about to forge paths into professional life, I think they're just as appropriate for those who are embarking on the Great Transition to retirement.

Here are the questions:

1. **"Wait, what?"** Commonly asked by incredulous teenagers, this question is actually a very effective way to gain clarity. It allows you to first stop and pause, then gain clarity and understanding so you can move forward. As you transition toward retirement, or any new phase of life, it's a question you should often ask to help you reflect in that process.

2. **"I wonder why?" (Or, "I wonder if?").** You're never too old or too experienced to be curious. Always look for ways to do things differently or make things better. You might ask yourself, "I wonder if we could ski every morning?" Or "I wonder why I feel like I have to work until sixty-five, just because the government and our culture say I should?" Or "I wonder what my perfect day in retirement looks like." As kids, we find it easy to imagine – but as adults – we often need permission to do so. This question helps in that.

3. **"Couldn't we at least?"** This question helps remove a barrier you might have. It also allows you to arrive at what's realistically achievable. "Maybe we can't afford to buy a beach house, but couldn't we at least afford to go to the beach two or three times a year to achieve the same experience?"
4. **"How can I help?"** The spirit of generosity is healthy and invigorating at any age. "Now that I'm going to have more time, how can I make an impact? How can I give back?"
5. **"What truly matters to me?"** This question requires a pause, and some reflection. What is it that truly matters to you? As you approach or are at your Freedom Day, how can you design a life that allows you to do the things you want to do? Don't let the simplicity of this question lessen in its impact. In fact, the answer to this question is the foundation to a great financial plan.

Ask yourself these questions, Ryan said at that 2016 Harvard commencement, and you'll also have the answer to a bonus question: "Did you get what you wanted out of life, even so?"

The questions are meaningful and important at any stage of life, not just graduation, and not just at retirement. The sooner and more frequently we can ask them, the better our chances are of getting what we want out of life, in spite of all the challenges and unexpected events that life throws at us.

The Great Transition will be different for each of us. Like my dad, you may have a business you wish to sell or hand over to the next generation in your family. Or maybe you want to put in just two more years into a career you've cultivated over time, then shift gears into a completely different encore career.

But it's important to understand that the move from working life into retirement is often a transition, as opposed to a hard stop. Navigating that transition, and then your retirement, requires planning, personal reflection, and asking a few key questions.

An investment advisor can help with the planning part.

What exactly is an investment advisor? Well, I'm glad you asked!

CHAPTER FIVE

What to Look for in an Advisor

The relationship between a client and an advisor can be remarkably unique and personal. As I noted, my father was surprised that, as a financial advisor, his clients often shared more sensitive details about their lives than members of his congregation shared with him when he was a Lutheran minister.

So, as you search for an advisor to help map out your Great Transition, it's useful to ask, what is it about yourself that would be most important for that advisor to know?

When meeting with potential clients, I often ask them to complete this sentence: "I wish I had an advisor with whom I could share _____."

That little exercise sparks a range of different concerns, from an engrained fear of spending money to a concern about having enough money to care for a surviving spouse. I've had some clients tell me, "Alex, I know I'm not going to be around for very much longer, and I want to make sure that I have my affairs in order."

The point is, finding the right advisor can be a little more personal than finding a good electrician or auto mechanic. With an advisor, you want someone who's working in your best interest over a long period of time, and with whom you can feel comfortable sharing the most pressing concerns and goals.

A good primary care physician, for example, is someone who knows you well, with whom you can share your most personal information, and who can formulate a care plan unique to your body and symptoms. You're likely not going to get the same level of personal care and expertise by occasionally checking in with an employee at the chain drug store around the corner.

Finding an advisor to help craft a financial plan for your future requires a similar approach and mindset to seeking out the right doctor.

However, before starting your quest to find the right advisor, it's important to fully understand the different kinds of advisors that are available to you in the financial services industry. To paraphrase an old *Sesame Street* song (yes, I have three young kids!), some of them are not like the others. The industry can be misleading about different financial professional roles, and what they can and cannot provide.

In this chapter, I'll explain what makes an investment advisor unique from other service providers in the industry. We'll also examine another commonly misunderstood term for those who are approaching or are in the middle of retirement — the "financial plan."

Three questions for advisors

We've all heard the term, "stockbroker" before. The term is pretty self-explanatory — the stockbroker fulfills your instructions by buying and selling stocks.

The advent of the internet, which allowed investors to do their own trading, made the role of a traditional stockbroker a bit of a dying breed. So, many brokers evolved into what is now known as a "financial planner."

What's unique about a financial planner is that it is not a regulated title. Because of that, virtually anyone in the financial services industry can call themselves a financial planner. Yet not all "financial planners" can legally give financial advice! How's that for confusing?

That's just one example of how challenging it can be to find the right advisor for your retirement goals and needs.

For the sake of clarity, I'm going to use the term "financial professional" to identify anyone in the financial industry. When interviewing a potential financial professional, there are some practical things you should know about the person you might choose to work with — and it is information that the professional might not voluntarily share. First, you should ask yourself, are you looking for an adviser to guide you with financial advice, or just a financial professional to help with transactions? Once you've answered that question, here are three key questions to always ask when meeting a financial professional:

1. How are you licensed?

2. Who do you work for?

3. How are you compensated?

These questions are crucial because the answers to these questions will tell you if the person you're dealing with is truly an advisor giving financial advice or just a financial professional selling a product. Does he or she receive compensation directly from you, or do they get paid through a commission from their company? Does this professional prioritize your goals and financial health, or is he or she a sales rep who is paid to market financial products that may or may not be in your best interest?

When seeking the help of a financial professional, there are generally two types of people you can meet:

1. People who are licensed to help you protect your money from loss.

2. People who are licensed to invest your money for growth, which involves market risk.

One example of a person who is licensed to keep your money protected is a banker. Banks are in the business of keeping money safe, right? This type of financial professional is employed and compensated by the bank.

Another entity on the guaranteed side of money is the insurance agent. They work for and are paid by the insurance company. When you purchase property and casualty insurance, you don't write the agent a check. The agent provides the product, you purchase the policy, and the agent is paid by the company, usually in the form of a commission. Insurance agents offer a range of products, including annuities and long-term care insurance. All of these products are designed, in some manner, to help protect your money or your assets.

So, if you talk to an insurance agent, they're going to want to keep your money protected, similar to a banker.

Now, let's look at those professionals who are licensed to handle the risk side of money management.

The first one is the broker, who might also be called a "registered representative." That means they're registered to sell you investment products. Who do they work for? They work for the company they're registered under — usually a brokerage firm, but sometimes a bank. Sometimes, they work for an investment firm like a mutual fund company.

How are these financial professionals paid? Not by you. You don't write a check to your stockbroker. They get paid by their company typically through a commission.

Finally, there's another role called the investment advisor. Like the broker, the investment advisor may also be licensed to provide stocks and securities and things like that. But there are a couple of important distinctions.

Investment advisors work with Registered Investment Advisory firms. That means they get paid directly by their clients. Some investment advisors might also earn a commission for the sale of insurance or investment products.

You know the old phrase, "Follow the money"? Following the money means that whoever is paying the money is the boss. Under the investment advisor model, the client is the boss, not some large financial services organization. Because of that direct relationship, the investment advisor has a fiduciary duty to their client. That duty, by law, means the advisor must act in the best interest of the client. It's the highest standard in the industry. When an investment advisor makes a recommendation, that recommendation has to be in the best interest of the client, not of themselves or the firm. All of the roles I described above may call themselves a financial advisor from time to time, which can be very confusing to the general public.

The title of investment advisor, however, is a regulated title. A banker or an insurance agent *cannot* call themselves an investment advisor. Currently, an investment advisor is the only license that requires having a fiduciary duty with the client. This means the advisor has to operate at all times in the best interest of you, the client. They must place your interests ahead of their own.

Banker	**Broker**
Insurance Agent	**Investment Advisor** **Fiduciary Duty**

To determine if the person you are speaking with is an investment advisor, you can ask to see their ADV form, which is documentation about the investment advisor and their business operations that is filed with either the Securities & Exchange Commission or the state securities authorities. An investment advisor is required by law to share their ADV with you and have you sign their client agreement when you engage their services.

More about investment advisors

So, as we've established, many in the financial services industry use different titles for the work that they do, from "planner" to "advisor." But think about that word — "advisor."

An advisor is someone who provides you with advice, right? Advice provided for a fee is an investment advisor. If you're looking for advice on where to put your assets and how to manage your money, you will probably want to look for an investment advisor. The other professionals are paid to sell you a product. There's nothing wrong with that, but you need to know how an advisor is paid, who they work for, and what's driving their interactions with you.

You might say to yourself, "Well, I'm perfectly comfortable crafting my own investment strategy and managing my money without handing things over to a third party." If that's the case, then you might not want to hire an investment advisor.

One way of looking at it is the relationship between the owner of a professional football franchise and the franchise quarterback. As the owner of your financial assets, you could choose to play the roles of both owner and quarterback if you want. However, you might choose to bring in someone else to do the quarterbacking — someone who's knowledgeable, who works for you and can follow your vision, but can carry it out in a way that allows you, as the owner, to focus on other things. The quarterback's job is to execute a game plan and to make sure that everything runs smoothly.

Most people that I talk to say emphatically either, "I do *not* want to be the quarterback." Or "I *no longer* want to be the quarterback." They want to spend time with the grandkids or pursue other interests, and not have to keep up with all the investment changes and strategies.

The investment advisor works for you. Like the quarterback, they're paid by you to use their skills and knowledge to execute an agreed-upon game plan.

As we know from watching pro football on Sunday afternoons, having the right quarterback can make the difference between winning and losing. While an investment advisor can't guarantee your investment performance, they can still be equally crucial in determining your success in experiencing the Retirement Zone.

But how do you find an advisor who not only provides advice and manages the day-to-day aspects of your investments, but helps you to understand how all of your assets fit together into a larger portfolio? Who can consult with you on issues like Social Security, taxation and insurance?

At LifePlan, we have thought about this. Here's how we make it work.

An advisor who wears multiple hats

So far, we've identified two kinds of advisors in the sometimes confusing world of financial services: those who keep your money safe, and those who are allowed to manage risk. The "safe money" people are insurance agents or bankers. The "risk money" people are registered representatives or investment advisors.

As we discussed earlier, investment advisors are the only ones who have a legal, fiduciary responsibility to provide you with investment advice.

However, even investment advisors are limited in the services they can provide.

Here's the problem with choosing to work with a financial profession who is only licensed as an investment advisor: they can only place your money at risk. For instance, you may ask them, "Can you help me understand long-term care insurance?" They're not going to analyze that and provide solutions. Let's say you want to talk to your investment advisor about a life insurance policy you have. They may say that they don't do that. But don't you think that insurance should be considered as part of your overall plan?

The problem with this situation is you may not get the most knowledgeable, customized advice for your complete financial picture. If a financial professional is solely an investment advisor, then they aren't licensed to help you with insurance. On the flip side, your insurance-only agent isn't licensed to provide investment advice.

Here's how we have solved that challenge at LifePlan Group: I have both licenses. I have my insurance license and I am an investment advisor. That's an important distinction. How can I be the best financial advisor to my clients if all I can do is help my clients with money in the market? That is why I also help our clients with their insurance needs.

Anyone who works with LifePlan has to use us as an investment advisor which creates a fiduciary relationship. We don't work with people only as an insurance agent.

We do not carry a brokerage license. We are not registered reps, and that's pretty rare. A lot of brokers are both. If you go to a big name brokerage firm, then there are certainly brokers, possibly also investment advisors. We choose not to have that license. We don't want to work for and be paid a commission by a brokerage firm or be told what products we can provide our clients.

At LifePlan, we choose to be independent financial advisors, providing us with the greatest flexibility in providing advice and direction to our clients. In addition to being an insurance agent, we find that this is the set-up that best allows us to do that.

License vs. designation

Regardless of whom you choose to work with in financial services, it's important that you make that decision with your eyes open, fully aware of that person's capabilities, motives and responsibilities.

Too many times, I hear about people who think they are speaking with an investment advisor who has a fiduciary responsibility to their clients, when in fact they are speaking with a registered rep who is compensated to sell them a product. That's like going to a Toyota dealership and expecting the sales manager to recommend the best possible car for your needs. What brand of vehicle do you think the Toyota rep is going to recommend?

One way to understand a financial professional's credentials is to determine what designations and licenses they have.

What's the difference? Many advisors will share with you that they are a CERTIFIED FINANCIAL PLANNER™ professional, or CFP® for short. This sounds like an official, legal license, but it's not. A CFP® is a designation. It's a membership, governed by a board, but the CFP® board does not regulate its members by law.

The CFP® requires training on a regular basis, and it shows that an advisor is serious about the work and continuing to gain knowledge about the profession. I have a CFP® certification myself, but the CFP® is not a license, and it should not be portrayed as such.[5]

---

[5] Certified Financial Planner Board of Standards, Inc. (CFP Board) owns the certification marks CFP® and CERTIFIED FINANCIAL PLANNER™ in the United States, which it authorizes use of by individuals who successfully complete CFP Board's initial and ongoing certification requirements.

There's a similar dynamic in the real estate industry. To be a real estate agent, you need to have a license through the state. However, to be a Realtor, as many real estate agents are, you just need to belong to a non-regulatory association. Therefore, there is a distinct difference between a real estate agent and a realtor.

This can be confusing, can't it? Even for me, it takes a lot to get a handle on all the different licenses and designations. The key takeaway is to first ask yourself who are you looking for. A financial professional to provide a product, or a financial advisor to give you comprehensive advice? If it's the latter – you want to look for an investment advisor.

Now that we have addressed some of the differences among registered representatives, investment advisors, and independent financial advisors, let's delve into another term that's commonly misunderstood in the financial services industry — the financial plan.

What is a financial plan?

"Financial plan" gets used very loosely in our industry and also with clients.

When I ask potential clients, "Do you have a financial plan?" most of them say yes, but that can mean a lot of different things. Some people think of their 401(k) at work as their financial plan. Others may believe they have a financial plan because they have different accounts in retirement savings.

But financial accounts are not the same as a financial plan.

Put simply, a financial plan is a written document that contains information on all your current finances, and future projections. For example, your financial plan will tell you when you're going to take income in retirement, and how much money you're going to draw from which accounts, and of course, the tax impact of those distributions. Your financial plan includes a holistic view of all your finances, and contains a tax strategy for pre- and post-retirement.

Don't let a financial plan be confused with an Investment Policy Statement, which is often provided from an advisor on how to invest your money in a particular account. While it is a necessary document to provide investment clarity, it's not a financial plan.

I think that's where people think they have a financial plan, and they really don't. A financial plan is almost like an architectural blueprint to build your dream home. It's detailed, well-crafted, and it's a picture of your future reality. When you look at renderings created by a good architect, you can see your future home, and you know what it's going to look like before construction.

Like the architect's blueprint, a good financial plan helps you to anticipate and envision the future. It can walk you through potential pitfalls, solutions, as well as what's going to happen to your money and thus the life you want to live. Like a blueprint of your dream home, the financial plan can be amended and altered to meet your specific tastes, and to adapt to conditions outside of the home. The plan is not static — it takes into account what's happening in your life and the larger world.

Here are a couple of examples of what a financial plan can do. A good plan will show when it is best for you to collect Social Security, how much you and your spouse will receive each year, and the impact that influx of money is going to have on your assets. It can tell you whether you're well-positioned to start taking Social Security at age sixty-two, sixty-five, or sixty-seven, or some other combination.

A good financial plan is able to tell you, "Yes, this is the best path for you."

This diagram illustrates the key components of any good financial plan.

Financial Plan
- Investment Management
- Tax Strategy
- Retirement Income Planning
- Estate & Legacy Planning
- Insurance Planning

Another example of how a financial plan works is related to required minimum distributions, or RMDs. Federal law has been updated to require that, at age seventy-two, you must start taking money out of your retirement accounts. Have you considered how much you'll be required to take? Or how it might affect your taxes? A good financial plan is going to tell you how much to take out, and it's going to tell you that well before you reach seventy-two so that you can be prepared for the impact. The plan can also advise on whether you should start taking money out before you reach seventy-two, and when you should adjust the level of risk in your investment strategy.

Another example: when a spouse dies, the surviving spouse gets the larger portion of Social Security payments, but the smaller portion goes away. How should the surviving spouse make up for that lost income? How do they prepare for that? What happens in the event that a spouse needs long-term care assistance? A good financial plan looks through all the components of financial planning and coordinates them to provide you with a written road map that can anticipate and adjust to meeting unexpected life events.

We call our financial plan the LifePlan Map™. When done right, the nuts and bolts fade to the background and the result is confidence and peace of mind to live the life your most wish to live!

At what age should you consider formulating a financial plan? Well, it's kind of like the flight of an airplane. When the plane takes off, the pilot knows where he wants the plane to land. When you start your career, you have an idea of when you want to retire, just like the pilot knows his destination. But on a long airline journey, the pilot doesn't keep the landing gear out the whole time. That would be impractical and unnecessary. In fact, the plane is probably on autopilot for much of the journey!

The point of this metaphor is, for the majority of your working career, you don't need a detailed plan for how you're going to balance distributions with Social Security in tax-efficient ways. You don't need to go through the landing checklist yet.

But, as you get closer to your destination, you better believe that the pilot of your plane is going through a lot of checks and adjusting a lot of controls. Likewise, on your journey to retirement, you need to start formulating the details of a financial plan within about ten years of when you plan to stop working. When you get to that ten-year window, you want to start going through your retirement checklist.

One of the mistakes some people make is that they don't really start thinking about retirement until they hit it. Can you imagine the pilot going through the landing checklist as the planes hits the runway! In order to have a smooth landing, you need to prepare. You need to talk to an advisor. You need to have a plan mapped out.

That doesn't mean that things don't change. A good plan is not static. It is not etched in stone. I think changes to your plan should always occur as you get closer to retirement, just as a pilot is doing everything possible to adjust to weather conditions, wind speeds, visibility, and other factors to ensure the smoothest possible landing. As you near your retirement, you need to make necessary adjustments to your plan.

An airline journey doesn't end once you hit the runaway. You still need to get to the gate — no one wants to be stranded out on the tarmac! Likewise, your financial plan doesn't end once you are retired. Throughout retirement you have to adjust your investments to be properly allocated for your changing needs. This assures that your journey throughout retirement is smooth and you enjoy your destination, the Retirement Zone, in the best way.

As I mentioned, some of us don't want to be bothered with retirement until it's breathing down our necks. I've had some potential clients tell me, "I'm not retiring for another year, and I'll deal with this then." And I tell them, "We don't have time. You can't retire and not have a plan."

On the other hand, though, it's never too late to start planning.

One client asked me once, "Alex, what is the best time to plant an oak tree?"

I shook my head. I had no idea.

"Thirty years ago," she answered.

She paused, perhaps for dramatic effect, then she asked another question: "When is the second-best time to plant an oak tree?"

I didn't know.

"Today," she answered.

The point is that financial planning and building a sound plan, take a long time.

But even if you've put off planning for your retirement, the next best time to start is today.

Where to keep a financial plan?

Once you have found your advisor and charted your route to retirement with a financial plan, one final question is, where do you keep your financial plan?

At LifePlan, we keep the plan in a secure, easy-to-access website with account balances updated daily for clients. We also provide a vault — a small, fireproof safe where clients can keep their estate documents, powers of attorney docs, insurance policies, identification, titles to their cars, and their deed to their house. We believe that there are three important places to keep the documents — one is in a vault at home, another is online in a secure portal, and the third is a USB thumb drive we provide for clients to put their most important emergency documents on. Those three areas should cover all your bases, if you will. And LifePlan provides our clients the key ring, the vault, and the website.

A really good blueprint is only good if it gets built. A good financial plan is only good if it's executed and you have the documents in the right places.

I hope this chapter has provided some clarity on the financial services industry and some of the key, but often misunderstood terms that get bounced around. Hopefully, this sparks some thoughts about what you want from an advisor and a financial plan. Having a greater understanding and more confidence will help you know what questions to ask an advisor, and help you live in the Retirement Zone.

CHAPTER SIX

Your Perfect Day

When I ask clients what their lifestyle is going to be once they retire, they often don't know how to articulate it to me. Most people have "bucket list" items for their retirement — to see Machu Picchu in Peru, or to finish that Great American novel, or to play golf at Pebble Beach.

But retirement consists of a lot more than those once-in-a-lifetime events you never got around to doing when you were working. During your retirement, when you aren't hiking to the bottom of the Grand Canyon or traveling across the country to see the grandkids, what are you doing? What does a typical, ordinary day in retirement look like? Better yet — what does the *perfect*, ordinary day look like?

Most people don't think about what they want to be doing, day in and day out, once they retire. They need a little prodding to envision it.

So I ask them a few questions. While you're reading this, I would also encourage you to answer along, or better yet, write down your answers to these questions.

First, I tell them, "I want you to close your eyes and envision a perfect day." Then I pause and ask them a question: "Where are you on this perfect day?"

They'll think for a moment, then reply with an answer. It can be anything from "I'm traveling," to "I'm at the beach in California," or even, "I'm in my backyard."

My next question is, "What are you doing? What is the activity on this perfect day?"

I might get an answer like, "I'm going for a walk," or "I'm enjoying a glass of wine," or "I'm chatting with my friends."

Then I ask, "Who are you with? Who is sharing this perfect day with you?" People will typically answer that they are with their spouse, their grandkids, or their friends.

The last question I ask is, "At the end of this perfect day, you turn out the light, and you go to bed. Can you describe to me at that moment how you feel?"

Clients respond with a range of emotions: "fulfilled," "grateful," "loved," — even "exhausted."

Those feelings that clients share with me in describing their perfect day — that's what I want the outcome of our work together to be. I want my clients to experience as many perfect days as possible.

The Roman Stoic philosopher, Seneca, wrote a famous moral essay called, *On The Shortness Of Life*. In it, he argues that most people spend their lives meeting obligations, putting in long hours at work, and competing with their peers for status — things that seem necessary, but bring little joy. Most of us feel like we'll ease up, relax and do the things we love when we're less busy and when we have more time. We'll stop to smell the roses eventually, but it'll have to wait a little while.

For many of us, that time never comes. Life flies by, and we spend much of it on matters that, in hindsight, seem mundane and trivial. As Seneca points out, we live as if we have a surplus of time when, in fact, we do not.

"You live as if you were destined to live forever, no thought of your frailty ever enters your head, of how much time has already gone by you take no heed," he writes. "You squander time as if you drew from a full and abundant supply, though all the while that day which you bestow on some person or thing is perhaps your last."

The main point? Life is short, so enjoy it as much as you can. The internet has hundreds of variations of the following quote, probably because it rings so true to so many of us: "No one ever said on their deathbed, 'I wish I spent more time at the office.'"

To quote another esteemed, well-known philosopher, Ferris Bueller, "Life moves pretty fast. If you don't stop and look around once in a while, you could miss it."

Now that you are envisioning a stage in life when you don't have to go into the office, when there are fewer stresses and obligations, you'll be able to focus on the activities and people you love the most. That requires a little vision and planning. Without thinking about how to concoct your perfect day, you may never get around to realizing it.

Of course, with most people, there are many different types of perfect days. I'll ask my clients to write down as many of those versions as they can imagine, and then ask themselves those four questions for each of those scenarios: Where am I? What am I doing? Who am I with? How do I feel at the end of that day?

Maybe one version of the perfect day is a vacation at the beach with your kids and grandchildren. If so, let's build that into the financial plan. How do we fund that vacation? Are your kids willing to pay for their airfare, or do you want to cover that expense?

The key is having complete alignment between your perfect days and your financial plan.

Even if retirement is still years away, it's never too early to envision what you want to be doing on a regular basis. If we don't ever define that perfect day (or days) and seek out a way to create more of them, it's very easy to let five years slip by until you realize you're still having the same kinds of days you've always had: routine, predictable, unfulfilling.

I ask my clients, "If we could figure out a way for you to have 10 percent more perfect days, or even 20 percent, would that make a difference to you?" And my clients always answer, "Yes."

The outcome of this exercise is to be able to experience more of life. Ideas must come from clients because every single client has a different concept of the perfect day. One perfect day could be woodworking in their shop. Perfect days don't have to be exotic or expensive.

The idea of envisioning the perfect day came to my father and me from our experiences working with LifePlan clients and talking with other advisors. It's the result of years of asking questions, listening to clients, and figuring out the most effective method for crafting days that are more fulfilling and then adjusting the financial plans to fuel them.

It can be very powerful, but not everyone will buy into this. Some will tell me they're already living every day perfectly which, when true, is awesome. But most clients seem to appreciate and value the reflection and purpose required to arrive at the perfect day. We have found that clients who go through this exercise often live the most fulfilling retirements.

Other ways of getting to the perfect day

Many clients engage in numerous conversations before realizing their perfect day. Once the advisor-client relationship has deepened, I'll often ask more specific questions.

One may be, "Does your current home fit your lifestyle as you continue to age? Is this your retirement place? Do you expect to live in your current home for the foreseeable future?" For many, our house can be one of our most expensive assets, and figuring out where it fits in a client's idea of a happy, meaningful retirement is important, particularly when thinking through the lens of aging and possible health changes.

Another question is, "If you could change anything about the way you were raised on how to handle money, what would it be?"

The reason I ask this question is because it aligns with the perfect day. Maybe your idea of a perfect day would be spending time in another city closer to your grandchildren, but that contradicts with your underlying beliefs and values on spending and managing money. So, we have this challenge, this preset notion of handling money blocking your way to living more of those perfect days.

Sometimes, I'll ask, "Is there something you've dreamed of doing for a long time?"

Then I'll pause before asking, "Why haven't you done it?"

The purpose is uncovering the roadblocks to the perfect day. We all have them.

As I mentioned, my grandmother jumped out of an airplane at age seventy-five. It's something she dreamed of doing for a very long time. Eventually, she realized that dream. But not all of us do. We put it off, and if we wait too long, we may find that we've exhausted that precious resource that Seneca talks about: time.

In my business, there's a strong connection between those perfect days, bucket list items and financial planning. If you don't plan and prepare for the lifestyle and events you want, they may never happen.

In the next chapter, I'm going to address some of the financial realities of retirement — taxation, Social Security, and required minimum distributions — and suggest some ways to avoid letting those challenges get in the way of realizing your perfect days.

CHAPTER SEVEN

Retirement Realities and How to Address Them

Every now and then, my wife Lauren and I make a shopping trip together to Costco. If you're a member of Costco or Sam's Club, then you're familiar with the experience of navigating a massive retail warehouse with towering shelves filled with consumer goods and food in bulk quantities. Sometimes, it can seem a little overwhelming.

Anyway, my wife and I push our oversized shopping cart up and down the aisle of Costco, occasionally stopping to put something in the cart to feed our hungry family of five. On one trip to Costco, we were almost finished with our shopping when Lauren had to take our daughter to the restroom. I agreed to check out our items and meet them near the front of the store.

So, I go through the checkout counter, make our purchase with my credit card, and I meet up with Lauren and my daughter.

"Do you remember what the bill was?" Lauren asked me. "Was it around $150?"

I stared at my wife in amazement. The total purchase was $147. Which, by the way, is a feat to get out of Costco for only $147!

"How did you know almost exactly how much it was?" I asked her.

As we made our way to the car, my wife explained that each time we put something in our cart, she made a mental note of that item's price, and added up in her head how much our total purchase would be. As I have learned, her estimate is rarely off by more than a few dollars.

I mention this story because retirement planning is a little bit like grocery shopping. Throughout your working years, you're putting things into your shopping cart. Instead of bananas, bread, and breakfast cereal, these items are financial products: 401(k)s, life insurance, and other investments.

When you retire, it can seem like going through the checkout line at Costco. You've selected these products, and now you're taking them out to be scanned. However, instead of a friendly clerk at the counter, it's the IRS. And the IRS is telling you what the taxes are on each of these items.

Here's the difference between grocery shopping and retirement planning. If you're at Costco and you're surprised by how much the bill is, you can always go back and put a few items back on the shelf.

Guess what? You can't do that with retirement income planning. Once you put money into a retirement account you can't take income out without paying taxes on it, it's purchased!

So, the questions you have to ask yourself when it comes to planning your retirement are twofold:

1. Do I know what's in my shopping cart?

2. Do I know how much it's going to cost?

That's the whole premise of this chapter about facing some of the financial realities of retirement. You need to know what you've purchased, and how much of a cut Uncle Sam is going to take. The earlier you know, the better. You might even be able to make changes still. To use the Costco example, you'd rather be surprised by the total bill when you're five-deep in line, rather than having the total tallied up at the checkout counter.

With that in mind, let's look at two of the most talked about — and commonly misunderstood — aspects of taxation during retirement: Social Security and required minimum distributions (RMDs).

Death, taxes, and Social Security

Imagine that you're putting together a jigsaw puzzle, and you start, as many of us do, by laying out all the pieces, face-up, on the table. Each of these pieces represent different financial components, and they're all related to one another. Put the puzzle together, and you have a complete picture of your financial plan for retirement.

One challenge many of us have, however, is that we think about each of these puzzle pieces in isolation. We don't grasp how they fit together to form the big picture.

Social Security is one such puzzle piece that people tend to fixate on. The big question about Social Security, of course, is when you should take it. Should you start receiving payments as early as sixty-two, or as late as seventy? Or maybe somewhere in the middle?

We all know that the longer you wait to start collecting Social Security, the larger the monthly payments will be. However, waiting until age seventy to collect might not be the best strategic move for everyone. The best time to draw Social Security depends on a range of factors. Like a single piece of a puzzle, you need to figure out how Social Security fits with the other pieces to form the complete picture of your financial plan for retirement.

Here are three key factors to keep in mind when thinking about Social Security:

1. Health and life expectancy
2. Taxation
3. The surviving spouse

It can be an uncomfortable topic, but how healthy are you? If you were to put a number on it, how long do you expect to live? If you're uncertain about how to answer those questions, it would be a good idea to consult your physician. If you don't want to wait until your next annual physical, there are scores of calculators on the internet. Just google, "life expectancy calculator." These sites typically ask a few simple questions about your health history and lifestyle, and can give you a ballpark estimate on life expectancy. As with anything on the internet, your mileage (and accuracy) may vary, depending on what kind of resource you use.

It's important to contemplate life expectancy because that information can greatly inform when you should consider collecting Social Security payments. If you're active, in good shape, and have a strong family health history, you might expect to live until ninety-five. Maybe you'll even live to be a hundred. After all, the number of centenarians in the U.S. is expected to reach a staggering 589,000 by 2060.[6] Suppose longevity appears to be in your future. In that case, it might be a good idea to wait until sixty-seven or seventy to start collecting, enabling you to max out your monthly Social Security payments.

However, you may not expect to live that long into retirement. In that case, why not start collecting Social Security at a younger age? If you think you would be lucky

---

[6] statista.com. 2021. "Number of people aged 100 and over (centenarians) in the United States from 2016 to 2060."
https://www.statista.com/statistics/996619/number-centenarians-us/

to live until seventy or seventy-five, you might consider collecting at sixty-two, the earliest eligible age, so that you enjoy the money you've contributed to the Social Security system while you are still leading an active life.

One thing most people don't consider when they mull over the distribution phase of retirement are the taxes they'll need to pay on their Social Security benefits. Almost no one factors in taxes. Yet, the Society of Actuaries recently published a report that said taxes may be the most important factor to consider when deciding someone should start taking Social Security.

Wait — what? Social Security is taxable? It wasn't always that way. For decades after Social Security was signed into law in 1935, it was tax-free. But people didn't live as long, or collect as much in Social Security, back in those days. So, in the early 1980s, Congress decreed that 50 percent of Social Security benefits could be taxable. In 1993, Congress passed a new law that stipulated that up to 85 percent of your benefits could be taxable.

Many people are surprised by the amount of their Social Security benefits that are taxable — and not surprised in a good way! What they don't realize is that Social Security is unique in that its taxability can vary — it's never 100 percent taxable. In fact, there's a formula the IRS uses to determine how much of your benefits can be taxed.

You can get a sneak peak of what percentage you'll owe in Social Security taxes by looking at your 1040 income tax form. Let me give you an interesting example of one factor in the formula most people miss: on line 2(a) is a field called "Tax Exempt Interest." These are typically things like municipal bonds and other holdings that are not subject to federal income tax.

Why do you report tax-exempt interest on your federal return? Why is the IRS interested in this? They care because that tax-exempt interest goes into the formula used to determine what percent of your Social Security will be taxed. It's a small thing, but something that a lot of people don't know about it, and one indicator of your tax exposure once you start collecting Social Security payments. Imagine having municipal bonds in your investment strategy for the purpose of not paying federal income tax, and yet, they are causing federal income tax!

The third factor that will impact your Social Security benefits is the issue of the surviving spouse. When a married couple retires, both spouses start collecting Social Security. When one of them dies, the surviving spouse will collect the larger of the two Social Security distributions. The other distribution will disappear. I explain this to clients with a simple rhyme: "The smaller check goes away, and the larger continues to pay."

This can be a big issue for couples, particularly if both spouses were bringing in close to equal amounts of Social Security. Suddenly, upon death, that income stream is nearly cut in half. How does the surviving spouse make up for that lost income?

One solution could be for one spouse to wait a little later to collect Social Security in order to maximize their benefits, while the other spouse starts taking benefits sooner. This "laddering" approach to taking benefits at different times can help soften the blow of less Social Security income for the survivor. The health and life expectancy of both spouses can also figure heavily in this calculation.

How RMDs work

As you probably know, a required minimum distribution, or "RMD," is the amount of money that the government requires people who are of retirement age to withdraw annually from an employer-sponsored retirement plan, a traditional IRA or a SEP (SIMPLE individual retirement).

Why does the government care how much you withdraw from your retirement savings? It wants to be paid, of course! Products like 401(k)s and traditional IRAs are tax-deferred retirement accounts. When you take RMDs from those accounts, you pay taxes on the amount you withdraw.

The good news is that RMDs are not a requirement until you reach age seventy-two. The amount you take out is a percentage of your total retirement savings in tax-deferred accounts, and that percentage changes as you get older.

The IRS has what is called a Uniform Lifetime Table, which provides a factor to calculate your RMD from age seventy-two onward. At seventy-two, the factor under current law is 27.4. At age eighty-two, it's 18.5. With each passing year, the factor for your RMD gets smaller, which results in you having to take out a larger and larger portion of your account.

How does this work? Here's a fictional example.

On Feb. 5, George turned seventy-two years old. He's now required to take an RMD. To do this, he looks up his total account balance as of Dec. 31 of the previous year. For the sake of simplicity and easy math, let's say that total was $100,000.

Now George takes that $100,000 and divides it by 27.4 — the factor for age seventy-two. He comes up with $3,649.64, which is about 3.6 percent of the account. That's the amount of money that George must withdraw — and pay taxes on — for his RMD at age seventy-two.

Next year, at age seventy-three, the factor will be slightly smaller (and thus the amount required slightly more) — 26.5 — and so George's RMD increases. And this process will continue each year for the rest of George's life.

The RMD taxes like regular wages. Whatever tax bracket you're in, that's the percentage you will pay on your RMD distribution. However, if you fail to withdraw an RMD, there's a stiff, 50 percent tax penalty.

Fortunately, there is some flexibility in how you choose to take these required withdrawals. You can break the annual RMD up and take withdrawals from your retirement funds on an annual, quarterly, or monthly basis. Also, the RMD amount does not need to draw from just one of your accounts — it's a percentage of all of your pre-tax retirement savings. So, depending on the types of retirement accounts you have, you can be a little strategic in which funds you take distributions from.

There's another way to handle RMDs and minimize your exposure to taxation. But you have to plan ahead and exercise that strategy before turning seventy-two. Once you're seventy-two, it's "game over" as far as RMDs are concerned.

Three buckets and the golden window

In case you haven't noticed, I like to break down the complexities of investing and retirement planning into simple metaphors that I hope we all can understand. It probably goes back to my days as a teacher, trying to get high schoolers excited about mathematics.

So here comes another metaphor! Imagine you have three buckets for your savings and assets. The first bucket contains funds and accounts that are taxable as ordinary income when you take money out. These are your tax-deferred accounts like 401(k)s and traditional IRAs.

The second bucket is filled with assets and savings that you pay taxes on as you go. These are things like your bank account, non-retirement accounts, and other investment accounts. The important part of this bucket is when you have long term capital gains or qualified dividends, the tax rates on these assets are more favorable than the rates on ordinary income.

Finally, the third bucket is your tax-free bucket. It contains accounts like a Roth IRA, a Roth 401(k), or life insurance. These are assets and savings that you've already paid taxes on, and they have the potential to grow tax-free. You'll be able to draw funds from them without a tax hit, if you follow their rules. Here's a visual to help you understand the three buckets.[7]

---

[7] Withdrawals from tax-deferred funds are subject to ordinary income taxes, and if taken before age fifty-nine and one-half, may incur an additional 10 percent federal penalty. Roth distributions are tax free if taken after age fifty-nine and one-half, and the account has been open for at least five years. Life insurance policy loans and withdrawals will reduce available cash values and death benefits, and may cause the policy to lapse or affect any guarantees against lapse. Additional premium payments may be required to keep the policy in force. In the event of a lapse, outstanding policy loans in excess of unrecovered cost basis will be subject to ordinary income tax. Tax laws are subject to change.

Ordinary Income Tax   **Capital Gains Tax**   **Tax-Free**

401(k)   **Investment Accounts**   **Roth 401(k)**
IRA   **Roth IRA**
                                                                                                           Life Insurance

When you're working, you are likely putting money into all three of these buckets. At that time, you may not think much about which buckets you're filling up. You might think, "I'm saving money, and that's good."

True enough. However, the ratio of how you fill your buckets is going to impact your level of taxation when you retire. Most everyone I meet with is very heavy in the first bucket. Sometimes they have as much as 90 percent or more of their assets in that bucket. That's because many of my clients are baby boomers who began saving for retirement in the 1980s, when tax-deferred products like the 401(k) and the traditional IRA became popular ways to sock away money for retirement.

When you reach retirement, however, the first bucket is the least favorable. That's the bucket with the most rules

LIVING IN THE RETIREMENT ZONE | 95

and taxes, and the one that causes the most problems for retirees. It's the one that your RMDs are drawn from.

Fortunately, there's a way to minimize the amount of money you have in that first bucket, but it requires some proactive planning and moving around of assets.

I call it the "golden window," which is the period of time from age fifty-nine-and-one-half until seventy-two. That's a twelve-and-a-half-year window when you're allowed without penalty, and for many people, it often makes the most sense to move your money among the three buckets to devise the most beneficial allocation before RMDs hit at age seventy-two. One example of this is a Roth conversion — moving money from a tax-deferred fund in the first bucket to a Roth IRA in the third bucket. When you make these conversions, they will be still be taxed as ordinary income. There's no way to avoid paying taxes on this retirement money. However, paying those taxes upon retirement when you are younger and in a potentially lower tax bracket is usually preferable to waiting until you have to pay taxes on RMDs.

This golden window of time is the best period to rearrange your assets in a way that benefits you for the long term. Waiting until your seventy-second birthday is too late.

At that point, the assets in Bucket 1 are locked in, and you'll start paying taxes on RMDs.

To minimize this impact, we have to understand your tax position during three stages of life: before age fifty-nine-and-one-half, after seventy-two, and in between those ages.

For instance, let's say before fifty-nine-and-one-half, you're in a very high tax position. Then you retire, and you're in a lower tax position. When you reach seventy-two, unless you make some adjustments among your buckets, you could be in an even higher tax position than you were pre-retirement because of RMDs. So again, that in-between time is often the right time to move money between the buckets.

I would prefer all of my clients to pay less taxes as they get older. In order to make that happen, it requires some proactive planning.

Ultimately, the best solution is usually to have a careful balance of assets among all three buckets. Most people want to have as little as possible in the first bucket, but enough to take advantage of low tax rates. Bucket 2 provides you with liquidity that can be taxed at the lower capital gains rate, and Bucket 3 is tax free.

Why not have as much money as possible in Bucket 3? Well, you don't want to end up in too high of a tax bracket at the front end, and you want to take advantage of the lower tax brackets in the future. Remember, our tax system is progressive. You fill up the lower tax brackets before you get to the high ones, and if you moved all of your money into Bucket 3 and never ended up using it, then you just paid more taxes than you needed to over the course of your life. It's a balancing act.

As with anything, it depends on the goals of the client, but I am a strong advocate of trying to have money in all three buckets.

As you already know, there are many financial products across all three buckets that will be marketed to you as essential ingredients of a successful and fulfilling retirement. These include mutual funds, life insurance, annuities, long-term care insurance, and on and on. But which of those products are the right fit for your specific retirement goals?

I'll cover the pros and cons of each of those popular retirement instruments in our next chapter.

CHAPTER EIGHT

Retirement Instruments: The Good and the Bad

When you think about it, our current American ideal of the "dream retirement" — walking on the beach, playing golf, traveling the world, enjoying lavish dinners with friends — is only a few decades old.

Before the Social Security Act of 1935, most people simply worked until they died. The average life expectancy back then was between sixty (for men) and sixty-four (for women).[8] The idea of putting money away so you could stop working and "enjoy your golden years" was completely foreign to most normal Americans.

That began to change as life expectancy increased, the federal government created social programs to help seniors, and many employers offered generous pension plans. In 1960, the world's first master-planned retirement community, Sun City, opened in the hot, dry Arizona desert. It was a resort-style development where people ages fifty-five and older could pursue lives of leisure and recreation. The developers of Sun City marketed it as a permanent vacation spot where you could buy a nice home, meet new people your age, and soak in the fun, sun, and relaxation.

Sun City was a huge success and soon inspired similar retirement communities throughout the country, particularly in the Sun Belt states. The modern-day image of a fun-filled, active retirement — golf, tennis, aerobic classes in the pool, fine dining, bridge club parties — became an aspiration for many American retirees.

---

[8] Infoplease. Feb. 28, 2017. "Life Expectancy at Birth by Race and Sex, 1930-2010." https://www.infoplease.com/us/population/life-expectancy-birth-race-and-sex-1930-2010

Fast-forward six decades, and the idea of a living a prosperous, care-free retirement has only intensified. For many Americans, a comfortable retirement seems like a birthright, along with life, liberty, and the pursuit of happiness.

Retirement communities aren't the only ones selling us on the dream retirement. The marketing push includes insurance and other financial services companies, which over the years have rolled various products and positioned them as "must-haves" to ensure a secure, trouble-free retirement.

In this chapter, I'm going to summarize the benefits and drawbacks of the more popular products, and I'll share a little bit about how they may or may not fit into your unique financial plan for retirement. All of the products I describe have their good points. However, some of them have been misrepresented in marketing and the media, and may not always be useful tools for everyone's retirement.

Retirement instruments

Maybe it's because I'm a trumpet player, but I like to think about financial products for retirement as various instruments in a larger symphony orchestra.

Because of my musical background, I love going to the symphony. I try to get to a performance early when the musicians are warming up.

When you hear an orchestra warming up, it's kind of a mess. The trumpets are blaring, the violinists are going through their scales and the notes don't fit together in a way that makes musical sense. Then, all of a sudden, it gets quiet. Then, the lead violinist comes out and makes a tuning note, and everyone plays the same note. Then it gets quiet again, and the conductor walks onto the stage. The conductor bows, turns his back to the audience, and then raises his hands.

With just a simple cue from the conductor, all of this music comes to life. It's beautiful, it's organized and it connects. You can feel the music flowing through you.

I believe this is also how a great financial plan works. All of your financial products are like instruments. A life insurance policy can be the flute, a 401(k) the violin, and so on. Look, I get it, maybe it's a stretch to compare a great financial plan to an emotional moving symphony experience, but remember, I'm passionate about this stuff!

The challenge comes when the instruments aren't coordinated. A knowledgeable and thorough financial advisor understands how financial instruments work in harmony, much like an orchestra when it plays in concert. When financial products do not work together, a mess can develop similar to an orchestra's tune-up prior to a symphony.

There are other analogies for this. I had one client compare her financial accounts to the junk drawer in her kitchen.

"I've got all this stuff," she told me, "and I have no idea how it all works together."

Like musical instruments, these financial products are only at their best when they work together. You can't buy one of these products and have a financial plan, just like you can't buy a violin and expect it to sound like a symphony orchestra.

Also similar to a symphony, you don't need all of these products at the same time. In a concert, not all of the instruments are blaring at once all the time. Sometimes, the string section is playing while the woodwinds take a break, for example.

The same thing goes for your financial plan. Despite what marketers might tell you, you don't need all of these financial products at all times. You want to create your own symphony, putting the various instruments together in a way that works well for you.

Two types of financial instruments

When considering the various financial 'instruments' that are available for your financial plan, I find that it's helpful to put them into two distinct categories: products that include guarantees and protection, and products that include risk.

Another way of thinking about these products is that they can be two out of three things. It's sort of like when you turn sixteen, get your driver's license, and you're excited to get your first new or used car. Your dad tells you to look for three things in a car: it can be fast, cheap, or reliable. The problem is, no car is all three of those things. It can be fast and reliable, but not cheap. It can be cheap and fast, but not reliable. It can be cheap and reliable, but not fast.

The bottom line: It seems you can only have two of the three qualities in any car you purchase. The same goes for financial products. These products can offer varying levels of protection, liquidity, or growth, but you can only have as many as two of those three traits with any single financial instrument.

What follows are capsules that describe different products for retirement. I'll explain the advantages and disadvantages of each instrument, and which of the three qualities (protection, liquidity, growth potential) you can expect from each one.

Let's start with the guaranteed products first:

Protection and guarantees

Bank savings account

Qualities: Protection (FDIC-insured), liquidity

Advantages: Savings accounts are guaranteed, liquid, and an essential product for emergency and unexpected expenses. Generally, you want to have enough money in your savings account to allow you to sleep at night. More specifically, about three to six months' worth of expenses is usually a suitable amount to keep in a savings account at all times.

Disadvantages: The money in a savings account is protected, but it doesn't really grow. You want to keep enough money in savings to have liquidity, but not so much that it annoys you that the money in that account is not keeping up with the rate of inflation.

Certificate of deposit (CD)

Qualities: Protection (FDIC-insured), some growth

Advantages: Offered by many banks, CDs provide more growth than a savings account, but the money in that account is less liquid. The money is protected, though — the government guarantees up to $250,000 per account title with any FDIC-insured bank.

Disadvantages: When interest rates are low, the growth in a CD account will be small.

Term life insurance

Qualities: Protection, guaranteed death benefit

Advantages: The purpose of life insurance is to provide a guaranteed death benefit to survivors when a member of the family passes. Typically, you'll have a term policy — life insurance that covers a certain benefit amount for number of years. For example, you may have a thirty-year policy that pays out $500,000 in event of your death during that term. That death benefit is typically significantly more than the premium paid into the policy, this provides "leverage" or growth on your premium in the event of a death. You can also get group life insurance from your employer. In addition to providing protection, life insurance can be an effective way to transfer wealth, tax-free, upon death. Often these advantages are most beneficial when working and should be re-evaluated as you get closer to and into retirement.

Disadvantages: There's no liquidity, no cash value, and there's no growth to the death benefit. And once your term is up — whether it's fifteen, twenty, or thirty years — your life insurance expires. What do you do then?

Universal life insurance

Qualities: Protection, growth

Advantages: Designed as a more flexible improvement upon the more rigid whole life policy, universal life insurance provides you with a life-long guarantee. The policy's cash value (which is your premium payments minus the amount needed to pay the policy's expenses) can actually grow. While universal life pays out a tax-free death benefit, you may be able to use some of that money before you die as income in the form of loans and distributions.[9]

Disadvantages: It's still life insurance, so the money you put into universal life is less liquid than with other products. You also have to medically qualify for universal life insurance and manage your policy's cash values to ensure it remains in force.

Long-term care insurance

Qualities: Protection, growth (if used)

Advantages: This product is very similar to a homeowner's policy. Instead of insuring your home, you're insuring your well-being. Long-term care insurance helps cover the potentially significant costs of assisted and nursing home living that often occur near the end of life — expenses that can run well over $100,000 a year. The big advantage to traditional long-term care insurance is that it provides a tax-free way to pay for those expenses and protect your other assets in the event you need care.

---

[9] Policy loans and withdrawals will reduce available cash values and death benefits and may cause the policy to lapse or affect any guarantees against lapse. Additional premium payments may be required to keep the policy in force. In the event of a lapse, outstanding policy loans in excess of unrecovered cost basis will be subject to ordinary income tax. Tax laws are subject to change.

Disadvantages: Similar to a homeowner's policy, the premiums you pay are not locked in and not guaranteed. As the cost of medical care rises, so too may the premiums on your long-term care policy. Having a qualifying event that allows your family to use the long-term care insurance coverage can be problematic, depending on the type of care and nursing facility involved. Another downside is most long-term care policies are "use it or lose it." What if you or your spouse never need assisted living? Then, that money is never utilized.

Combination life with long-term care insurance

Qualities: Protection, growth

Advantages: Combination life with long-term care is exactly as it sounds. It's a life insurance policy that allows you to accelerate the death benefit while you are living to fund long-term care, tax-free. This flexible approach is beneficial due to the fact that an estimated 70 percent of seniors will need some form of assisted living during their lives.[10] However, if you're among the 30 percent who don't need long-term care, this insurance provides a death benefit.

---

[10] Saint Simeon's. "The Latest Assisted Living Facts and Statistics." https://saintsimeons.org/blog/the-latest-assisted-living-facts-and-statistics/

Disadvantages: The disadvantages of putting money into a combination policy are lower liquidity and potentially less growth than other uses of the premium, and again, you have to qualify medically — and will be subject to surrender charges. Do you need to have a form of long-term care insurance to pay for assisted living or a nursing home? Absolutely not. You can self-insure and pay out-of-pocket for those expenses. Whatever you decide to do, the prospects and likelihood of needing long-term care should be addressed somewhere in your financial plan.

Fixed and fixed index annuities

Qualities: Protection, growth

Advantages: Let's say you want the assurance of protecting your assets from market risk, but you don't want to wait for a catastrophe to happen to use that money? Well, there's always the fixed or fixed index annuity, which is an insurance product that provides protection of principal and guarantees. You take some of your assets, place them into an annuity, and it can provide guaranteed income and interest growth. It is a way to help protect a portion of your assets from stock market losses. One of the disadvantages of having a traditional pension is the flow of money stops when you die. When set up properly with an annuity, you get guaranteed income during your life and, if you die early, that remaining asset goes to your beneficiary. Many annuities also contain riders (often at additional cost) that can increase your income distributions during times of poor health.

Disadvantages: An annuity can provide better growth potential than some other low-risk investments like a CD. Even though the credited interest can be tied to stock market indexes (with a fixed index annuity), you likely won't have the same upside rates of return the market provides. This is a disadvantage if you are trying to maximize growth. Liquidity can also be a disadvantage of annuities. Often, you can only access chunks of money from the policy at a time or be assessed a surrender charge, and you may be limited in how much you can use. There may also be penalties for withdrawals before age fifty-nine and one-half. So, you get protection and the potential for growth with an annuity, but not easy access to cash.

Growth and risk instruments

Now, let's look at some of the products that enable a potentially higher rate of return on your money, but also include more risk.

Variable annuities and variable life insurance

Qualities: Growth potential, a level of liquidity

Advantages: Did you think all insurance policies were protected? Guess again. Variable insurance products are designed for consumers who are willing to assume a little more risk in exchange for a potentially higher return. These products are especially popular with higher earners who want to put some of their money in a financial vehicle that is tax deferred.

Disadvantages: Because they are tied to the ups and downs of the market, variable insurance products can lose money. The protection of your money is not guaranteed and the liquidity may vary. Another problem is many variable products include relatively high fees that are not always disclosed clearly to clients. Sometimes clients mistakenly think their variable insurance protects their principal from market loss like other insurance policies, this is not the case. Finally, while you receive tax-deferral on the growth, you do not benefit from lower capital gains rates. Instead, the growth is taxed as ordinary income (higher rates) and annuities do not receive a step up in basis at death to beneficiaries. As any annuity you may be subject to surrender charges.

Individual stocks

Qualities: Growth potential, liquidity

Advantages: Investments into individual company stocks can offer the opportunity for the greatest return on your money. They also come with the greatest risk of losing money. Some of this risk can be offset by investing in multiple types of stocks: from solid blue-chip stocks that pay a strong dividend, to mid-cap or small-cap stocks that carry greater risk, and a chance at greater rewards — but there is no guarantee.

Disadvantages: To truly mitigate risk in a portfolio comprising only of stocks, you'll need to own between twenty-five and thirty stocks in each asset class, in my opinion. That's a lot to manage. Building stock portfolios can be complex, requiring a lot of time, expertise, and attention. And, of course, your money does not have guarantees and is at risk of loss.

Individual bonds

Qualities: Growth potential, a level of protection

Advantages: With a stock, you own part of a company. With a bond, you are part of a group of investors providing a loan. A bond is called a debt instrument. Bonds are designed for slow, steady growth, and there's typically less risk to them than with stocks. Bonds also have a timeline to be paid back in full — it can be five years, ten years, or even twenty years. The level of risk depends on who is borrowing the money. If it's a start-up company, there's likely more risk. If it's the federal government, it's a safer bet you'll get your money back, plus interest.

Disadvantages: One of the bigger problems with bonds is liquidity. Let's say you purchase a ten-year treasury bond. What if you need to use that money before the ten years are up? You would have to sell the bond on the market and, depending on where the current borrowing rates are at, you could see a loss or a gain.

Mutual funds

Qualities: Growth potential, liquidity

Advantages: Mutual funds are popular because they provide greater diversity than just owning a couple of stocks or bonds. The funds are a collection of stocks or bonds put into one package. It's a pooled investment that's professionally managed and owned by a large number of people. There are hundreds of mutual funds to choose. Many of them have been around for several decades, and they can range in their level of risk. They can also be easily bought and sold to provide access to the proceeds for money needs.

Disadvantages: Because they are professionally managed, mutual funds often involve fees and some can be quite expensive. When you invest in a mutual fund, you have no control over the management of that portfolio of bonds and equities. You are trusting an unseen expert or algorithm to manage your money in that fund. Even though mutual funds are often well-diversified, they, too, carry a risk of loss.

Exchange-traded funds (ETFs)

Qualities: Growth potential, liquidity

Advantages: Like the mutual fund, an ETF is a collection of stocks and bonds. You can actively trade it on the exchange, so it's a little more liquid than a mutual fund. These funds can be professionally managed, or they can be index funds. The most famous index fund is the S&P 500, which is popular because it provides a wide range of stocks to ensure greater diversity: 500 of the largest U.S. companies.

Disadvantages: Similar to the mutual fund, an ETF is prepackaged and may not be the perfect fit with your investment strategy. While typically they have lower fees than mutual funds, some ETFs have high investment fees. The money in these funds is also tied to stock market performance, so there is risk involved.

Separately managed accounts (SMAs)

Qualities: Growth potential, liquidity

Advantages: The SMA combines all of the "risk" products into one account. It can include stocks, bonds, mutual funds, and ETFs. The account is professionally managed by an advisor. The convenience of the SMA is that someone else is managing your portfolio, and you don't have to get caught up on the details of investing in and diversifying your portfolio. Because this is an account specific to you, you can customize it to your desires and goals and tax manage it much easier than mutual funds or ETFs.

Disadvantages: The big drawback of SMAs is that they typically have higher account minimums to invest in this type of strategy. Because this is a custom account specific to you, it requires more time for the financial professional to manage, so there also might be higher managements fees.

How do these all fit together?

In the next chapter, I'll talk more about how you can begin to put some of these products together as you start to form your unique financial plan.

Again, you likely will not need all these instruments to assemble your symphony. Some of them you may never need. However, as you save for retirement, there are few general rules to keep in mind:

Know your investment philosophy. Before assembling a financial plan, it's important to think through your approach and comfort level with investing. Do you want a professional guiding you or handle everything yourself? Is your style to actively pick stocks and/or time the market, or would you rather take a more passive approach and invest in a portfolio or stock indices? Are there specific companies you wish to invest in, and others you would like to avoid? Is socially aware investing, often referred to as ESG, something that is important you, or not? Do you want your money to back certain causes or values that are important to you?

Diversify. The biggest red flag I see with potential clients is if they have close to 100 percent of their assets tied up in only one of these products. Maybe they have a portfolio made up entirely of stocks. Perhaps they have funneled all their savings into an annuity. Putting all of your money into one kind of product is never a good idea. It heightens risk and reduces opportunities.

Be mindful of risk. The best indicator of the amount of risk you are taking is the percentage of stocks and bonds in your portfolio. Historically, a "balanced" portfolio has been one that consists of 60 percent stocks and 40 percent bonds. How we approach risk at LifePlan is through an acronym: CAN. It stands for Capacity, Attitude, and Need. Capacity is, how much risk can you afford to take? Attitude is, what is your appetite for or comfort with risk? As for Need, what level of risk do you need to meet your goals? If you've saved very well, you may not need a lot of risk to make your plan work. A good investment strategy satisfies each part of the CAN acronym. While you will have an overall risk profile based on CAN, your plan needs to go deeper than that, which is where many plans fall short. To achieve your overall appropriate risk, that does not mean each of your accounts have this same level of risk. Often, accounts you will draw from sooner should be more cautious. Accounts not tapped for income for years, or never, should be more growth oriented. As with almost anything I discuss in this book, however, your mileage may vary. Depending on your age, income and goals, a portfolio that's riskier and heavier in equities might be the appropriate move.

Age matters, but it's not everything. Many people subscribe to the idea that, once you reach retirement age, it's time to put all your assets into bonds, CDs, insurance, and other conservative products to protect your money from a drop in the market. However, you *still* need your money to grow, especially if you have another twenty, thirty, or even forty years of life ahead. Taking an "all or nothing" approach to managing risk in your portfolio, regardless of your age, is rarely an effective strategy.

Bear markets do happen sometimes. Aside from the quick fall and rise during the early days of the COVID-19 pandemic, the stock market has grown steadily since March

2009 when a recovery began coming out of the global financial crisis. That track record of success makes it harder for us to understand risk, and how much money we can afford to lose if there's a downturn in the market. And bear markets do happen. Ask anyone whose portfolio took a hit during the financial crisis of 2008. When managing your portfolio, always keep in mind how protected your money is from severe fluctuations in the market.

Find your sweet spot. I often say that retirement is like walking a tightrope. You want to find that sweet spot between spending more money than you can afford, and not spending enough money to enjoy your life.

The same thing can happen with investing. You can take on too much risk, or too little. As you consider the myriad products that are out there for growing or protecting your assets, you need to find that sweet spot of risk and return. Lean too far in one direction or the other, and you can quickly get yourself into trouble.

CHAPTER NINE

Your Symphony: A True Financial Plan

As you now know, I've dedicated a large portion of this book to writing about the various puzzle pieces that go into a financial plan. We've covered how important it is to envision the kind of retirement you want before determining how to pay for it. We've covered the various types of financial professionals you may run across in planning for retirement. We've examined Social Security, RMDs, and the myriad financial products available to you to help secure a comfortable retirement.

Now, it's time to examine how to put these puzzles pieces together into a true, comprehensive financial plan.

Why is a financial plan important? Because without one, you have no overarching strategy for how you want to prepare for and fund retirement. You have only a collection of products — various tactics for retirement that may or may not fit together well. Going back to that favorite quote from one of my clients: you have "a junk drawer full of a bunch of stuff."

The great leaders of world history understand how important it is to have a strategy. Here's what Sun Tzu, the ancient Chinese warrior, and strategist, had to say about that subject in his legendary text, *The Art of War*: "Strategy without tactics is the slowest route to victory. Tactics without strategy is the noise before defeat."

In other words, tactics get the job done, but they're ineffective without strategy. Think about how the United States has fared in various wars over the decades. In World War II, the strategy was clear: deploy every possible resource to defeat fascism and depose its leaders. It took a mammoth amount of effort and sacrifice on the part of the Allies, but the mission was never in doubt, and the Axis powers were eventually defeated.

In the more recent Gulf War, the goal among the U.S. and our allies was more complex and not necessarily agreed upon. Once Saddam Hussein was defeated, there was no clear path for how to build a new government for Iraq, and then withdraw troops from the country. In short, we were effective in our military tactics — winning every major battle of the Gulf War, but there was no grand strategy of what to do after Hussein, and a long, drawn-out conflict with no clear winner was the result.

As you prepare your financial plan, I want you to have the best tactics available for you to deploy. But you also need a clear, consistent and broad strategy that's also flexible enough to respond to unexpected events. I want you to "win" retirement, and a financial plan is the fastest route to that victory.

Putting the pieces together

When considering how to assemble a financial plan, I find it helps to think of it in the same way you put together a large, challenging jigsaw puzzle.

In piecing together a big puzzle in the most efficient way, there are steps you need to follow. First, you turn all the pieces face-up, so you can see what you've got. Then, you identify the corner pieces. Then you work on the edges.

Then, once you have the frame of the puzzle complete, you start piecing together the picture inside.

I'm sure there may be other ways to tackle a complex, intricate puzzle, but those are the basic steps I learned when I was a kid. Without them, solving the puzzle would have been much more challenging, and would have taken much more time.

Similarly, there are steps involved in methodically piecing together your financial plan. Without these steps, planning for retirement can seem rudderless and chaotic — a bunch of stuff in a drawer. The good news is, we believe there are only seven steps you need to take to overcome this financial confusion and ambiguity, and ultimately, succeed in living in the Retirement Zone.

If you want to take the next step and not only read through these steps, but actually put pencil to paper and start putting the building blocks together for your own financial plan, I've provided worksheets at **www.LifePlanGroup.com/retirementzone** that you can use to follow along, and then download and print your notes as a PDF.

Step 1: Envisioning your retirement

When you retire, what you do you want to do? How do you want to live your life? This step goes back to "the perfect day" and other exercises I've shared to help articulate what retirement looks like to you. To plan for retirement, you need to be able to see the full picture — just like that image on the puzzle box that you'll refer to over and over as you assemble your puzzle.

I would suggest not only envisioning this, but also writing it down! We create what we call the LifePlan Torch for our clients. It is a written statement about the purpose of their money – the guiding vision of who they are and what they want their retirement to be. Consider the following prompts to help you come up with your guiding statement.

- To have the joy and peace of mind knowing that I (we)…
- It would be awesome to…
- I know I am financially free and independent so that I may…
- My resources are a tool to help me…

If you are still having difficulty really envisioning the types of activities you will do on a day to day basis in retirement – consider your interests. What do you like doing now? Ask a spouse or a friend, "What am I doing when you see me most excited and joyful?" Keep a journal – when you find yourself doing something you really enjoy, write it down. Often in retirement when you have more time to explore your interests, they turn into passions, and spending time in our passions results in living in the Retirement Zone.

Once you've conceived your unique vision for retirement, only then can you begin to examine how much it will cost. Remember, we call this "A" dollars. When you've arrived at how much money you will need to fund your ideal retirement — and the gap between what you'll receive from Social Security or a pension and the money you'll need to pull from other sources — you'll be ready to move on to the next step.

Step 2: Turning the pieces face-up

Now that you know what retirement looks like, and how much it will cost, it's time to open up the box, turn over the pieces and see what you've got.

You need to have a handle on all your financial accounts and their location: 401(k)s, Roth IRAs, traditional IRAs, life insurance policies, and so on. You need to know who owns these accounts (you or your spouse), the amount of money in each account, current beneficiaries, and its level of risk and return. Some financial instruments may be conservative, while others are more growth-oriented. And then there's Social Security. It's not an investment that includes risk, but it's an account you've been putting money into that will be a form of income when you choose to use it.

While reviewing all of these assets, it's important to identify which ones are income-producing and which ones are not. For example, your home and your car are assets, but they are not producing income for your retirement. A rental property, however, is an asset that might be a source of income for retirement.

At LifePlan, once we have worked with a client to identify all assets and sources of income, we put all of it into an account summary — an inventory in which we list all of them out. That makes it much easier to see your full outlay of assets in one location, calculate the income and level of risk, and identify any potential gaps in building your financial plan.

This account summary can be extremely revealing — and surprising — for the client. Just to give you one fictional example: let's say you have a Roth IRA that includes a growth-oriented mutual fund that's heavily invested in the telecom industry. Upon examining your accounts, you learn that your spouse's 401(k) has the exact same mutual fund that makes up more than 20 percent of the assets of that account. There's nothing terribly wrong with that, but it's a sign that your overall inventory of assets is not necessarily as diverse and balanced as it could be, or maybe that position isn't in the right tax "bucket" that we discussed in Chapter 7. That's the kind of thing you can learn when you assemble an account summary of everything you own.

Step 3: Determining your income base

Now that you have all your puzzle pieces face-up, it's time to see how they fit together, starting with the corners and the edges.

More practically speaking, it's time to determine how much income you can count on to help fund your retirement.

The two main pieces are Social Security and (if you have them) pensions. Another component, if you're still working, is earned income. Finally, there may be another asset providing you steady income. That might be a rental property or a generational family trust.

Put simply, anything that produces steady income that you can count on — that makes up your income base.

A lot of factors go into determining your income base. A good place to start is by deciding when and how to start collecting Social Security. Should you collect sooner or later? At LifePlan, this is where we pull back the curtain in looking at taxes, income needs, other owned assets, and life expectancies. All of these things will point toward a specific strategy for taking Social Security — a strategy that's very personalized and different for each person.

As I have mentioned before, it doesn't always make sense to wait until age seventy to start collecting Social Security and maxing out your benefits. Let's say you want to retire at age sixty-five, but not collect Social Security until seventy. How are you planning to fund those years between sixty-five and seventy, when you are younger and more active than you will be in later years? Does it make more sense to start collecting at sixty-five, when you're newly retired and can put that income toward travel or other activities you had envisioned for retirement?

Taxation of your Social Security payments is another consideration when determining the optimal time to start taking those benefits. Not all of Social Security is taxable, and that percentage can vary from one individual to the next. In planning when to take Social Security, you want to do it in a way that is the most tax-efficient.

Finally, there's the concern that you may actually collect less in Social Security if you wait until later to take it. Right now, the Society of Actuaries and the Social Security Administration estimate that, by the year 2034, Social Security will start paying out 78 cents on the dollar unless more funding for the program is provided.[11] Will Congress actually let that happen in 2034, or will it do something like raise payroll taxes to pump more money into the system? Will the normal retirement age for Gen Xers and millennials be raised to seventy in order to sustain Social Security? This all remains to be seen.

There are other questions to resolve when determining your income base. If you have a pension, do you take it single life, or joint life? Do you take it as a lump sum?

If you don't have a pension, what other streams of steady income can you rely on to help fund retirement? You want to write all of these down and add them up to arrive at an annual income figure for the next thirty to forty years. Make sure to determine this number year by year, include any cost of living benefits (COLA) that maybe provide, because as we have discussed, retirement isn't static. Your income base will likely change year by year and certainly when life events happen like the death of a spouse.

Then, it's time to determine the gap between your actual income, and the amount of money you'll need to fund your perfect days of retirement.

---

[11] Kenneth Terrell. AARP. Sept. 1, 2021. "Social Security Trust Funds Could Run Short by 2034 as Pandemic Takes Toll." https://www.aarp.org/politics-society/government-elections/info-2021/social-security-trust-funds.html

Step 4: Minding the gap

Now that you have a better feel for the amount of money you'll be bringing in during retirement, it's time to calculate whether or not that amount falls short of your intended retirement lifestyle. In most cases, there is a gap between the amount of steady income retirees can count on, and the cost of maintaining their lifestyle.

To use an example from an earlier chapter, if you need $100,000 annually to live a satisfying retirement and your base income is $60,000, your gap is $40,000. By the way, you'll want to examine and adjust this gap on an annual basis, so that you can factor in things like inflation. Assuming an annual inflationary rate of 2 percent, that $100,000 you're living off of today may look more like $104,000 two years from now.

The gap is where we find out how much you need to depend on your assets. While you're still working, your income gap is most likely positive, unless you downsized to a part time or lower paying job. You're likely making more money than you need, which enables you to put some of that money into retirement savings. After you retire, you'll likely be facing a deficit between income and lifestyle, and you'll need to start taking money out of those accounts in order to supplement your retirement income.

One other thing to consider is that the gap may be wider or narrower during different stages of retirement. For example, you might want to front-load your retirement spending during the first ten years, so you can go on big trips and have other experiences you never had time to pursue when you were working. Maybe the first ten years of retirement look more like $115,000 annually instead of $100,000.

I've also known people who actually spent more money in their later years of retirement. My wife's grandmother spent the early part of her retirement caring for her husband, who had dementia. When her husband passed, she was able to spend more money on trips and other activities that she was unable to do when she was caring for him.

The bottom line: we can't always predict where life will take us, but the likelihood of spending the same steady amount every year for the rest of your life is slim.

Step 5: Tax time

Now we're getting into the meat and potatoes of retirement planning: mapping out income from your retirement accounts to fill the gap and also pay your taxes.

This involves keeping a close eye on all of your accounts and determining which ones can provide income with the least amount of tax exposure. Remember the three buckets I described in Chapter 7? This is that period of time, between ages fifty-nine-and-one-half and seventy-two, when you can move money around among those buckets so that you aren't suffering a big tax hit when you start to withdraw that money later on in your retirement.

Figuring out the most tax-efficient way to withdraw money out of your accounts may sound cumbersome, but it can also be empowering. Knowing how much you're going to pay in taxes on withdrawals (and later, on RMDs) eliminates a lot of uncertainty. It gives you the security of knowing how much you'll owe in taxes, and how to plan around that to experience a satisfying retirement.

Step 6: Making the money grow

Once we have figured out where the money is going to come from to fund your retirement, we are ready to move on to the next step: how do we invest that money in order to achieve your retirement goals?

Most financial advisors will start with this step. I think that's a mistake.

Before knowing where and how to invest your money, you need to know what you want to do during retirement, how expensive that lifestyle may be and how much money you have available to pay for it.

We covered all of that in Steps 1 through 5. Now, in Step 6, we examine the risk and returns of each of your accounts, and identify the retirement instruments you need to put together to assemble your "symphony" of a retirement plan. In this step, you're determining your investment philosophy and policy statement for each account. For those accounts you rely on sooner for income, you'll want the philosophy to be more conservative. For money that's not needed right now, but later on in your life, you can probably afford to be more aggressive and growth-oriented.

At LifePlan, we often consolidate a client's number of accounts, ensuring a simpler approach to getting the job done. Let's say you have ten different retirement accounts. Is it possible to narrow those accounts to four or five, and achieve the same, if not potentially better results? Often, it is. Really, you may want to have the fewest number of accounts to achieve your investment goals. Simpler is better.

This is also a time when you might add a new instrument or two to your retirement symphony. Maybe there's an income annuity you'd like to add, or some other investment outside of your 401(k). Now might be a good time to meet with a professional to find the best way to accomplish this.

In a way, Step 6 is kind of like going through your attic or storage rooms, and getting rid of some of the stuff you don't need. As the Japanese organizing consultant Marie Kondo likes to say, if something doesn't "bring you joy," get rid of it. Similarly, if the old 401(k) account you still have from three employers ago no longer fits into your investment philosophy, roll that money into a better account.

Once you're finished with Step 6, congratulations! You now have a basic financial plan that should check all of the boxes as they pertain to your income needs and tax strategy.

Now, it's time to put that plan to work.

Step 7: Implementation

Until you begin executing it, your retirement plan is only as good as the paper it's written on. Step 7 is where you begin to make changes to your accounts. You look at your retirement investments and start making adjustments according to your new plan.

Once you have implemented your investment strategy and after your income needs have been addressed, it's time to consider the uncertainties of life. What happens if something unexpected occurs — a health issue, the loss of a spouse, a family member who needs financial help? Is your financial plan going to address issues like life insurance and long-term care, or do you need to meet with professionals to come up with some additions to your plan?

This is also the point where you carve out some time to think about estate planning. Do you have your will in order? Your estate documents? A designated trustee or a power of attorney? Do you have goals in mind for charitable giving or an inheritance for your children once you pass? Are all of your account beneficiary designations coordinate tax efficiently with your eventual estate?

This is what I like to call "Phase 2" of financial planning — the more advanced stage when we determine other things to add to your plan that will sustain you and your retirement through life's unexpected events.

In most cases, you have plenty of time to address these future, long-term concerns. What's important at this moment — Step 7 along the journey — is that you now have a functioning, comprehensive financial plan that is working toward your retirement. You have put the puzzle pieces together to form the larger picture of what retirement looks like, and how you are going to fund it.

One last step!

One more crucial step: now that you have a financial plan, don't just set it aside and ignore it. Ideally, you should review and make any necessary changes to your plan on at least an annual basis or whenever big, life-changing events come up.

As you already know, life doesn't always go according to our wishes. Life changes. Laws change. Taxes change. I've never created a financial plan that I haven't changed.

So just keep in mind that, even after you've done the heavy lifting of creating a financial plan for retirement, the work continues. As time goes on, you'll need it to be dynamic, flexible, and able to change as your life changes.

CHAPTER TEN

The Retirement Zone

Shortly before his death in 1980, John Lennon wrote and recorded a song called "Beautiful Boy (Darling Boy)," which the former Beatle dedicated to his young son, Sean. There's a lyric from that song that has stuck with me over the years: "Life is what happens when you're busy making other plans." It's actually a quote that was first popularized by the writer and cartoonist Allen Saunders in a 1957 issue of *Reader's Digest*.

It's a quote that resonates because it happens to be true. While we plan and scheme for the future, whether it's pursuing a new career, planning a move to a different city, raising our kids or planning for retirement, life keeps happening. Life doesn't always mirror our dreams and ambitions and, as the philosopher Seneca pointed out, we often go through our lives as if we have a surplus of time. In fact, time is the most limited and valuable asset each of us possesses.

So, what's the point of having a financial plan if life just "happens?" My hope is, if you take the time to pull together and maintain a cohesive plan for funding your retirement, this will free you up to enjoy more of life. I want for you to have more meaningful moments and perfect days because you aren't worried as much about money, the coming years, and how you can continue to afford and enjoy a comfortable lifestyle with the ones you love. Reducing worry can generate the energy and creativity to intentionally live your best life!

In our fast-paced world of social media and twenty-four-hour news networks, it's easy to be overwhelmed by too much information about the stock market, politics, and world events. My father sometimes talks about how, when he was growing up, the newspapers didn't report the stock market performance on a daily basis — they reported it once a week. Can you imagine that in today's world? Now, of course, you can track stock prices on a minute-by-minute basis, but do you want to do that? Is that really healthy? Does it even matter?

The idea behind a financial plan is you don't need to obsess about what's happening in the market or the world at large. The plan is there to execute your strategy for income and investing and, if you work with an advisor, you have a quarterback who's executing the plan, a conductor who is guiding the symphony, a coach ensuring you are living in the retirement zone!

Are there times when the market corrects itself, or an unexpected life event occurs, and you need to modify your plan? Certainly. You'll need to work closely with your advisor when the unexecpted occurs.

Generally, however, checking in annually with your advisor to go over the plan, confirm annual tax strategies, and make adjustments is fine. You can certainly have quarterly or even monthly touch-bases with your advisor if you want. The ideal scenario is that you look at your plan's performance often enough to give you peace of mind, but not so often that it gives you anxiety.

When I meet up with a client for our annual strategy session and review of their financial plan, we often talk more about what's happening in their lives than we talk about the financial instruments. We discuss the life they want to live, what they're accomplishing now, and what they want to do in the future.

Having those kinds of conversations is often a sign that you have a really good financial plan. Instead of pouring over numbers and the rates of return, you're focused on your life and what you want to do next. You know the resources are there to live the life you want, so you're not too concerned about the annual yield on that mid-cap fund in your portfolio over the past twelve months. What's more important is knowing you're on track to meet your most important life goals.

I recently met with clients who were marking their fortieth wedding anniversary in 2021. They had envisioned taking a long, international trip to celebrate this momentous event in their lives. Of course, the COVID-19 pandemic changed those plans, and they ended up doing a more modest domestic trip. So, like it was for many of us during the pandemic, there was a tinge of disappointment in our conversation that my clients could not do everything they wanted.

At no point in our chat, however, were there concerns of, "Can we afford to do this?" or "What are the consequences of spending money on an expensive trip?" It was more about the importance of this couple celebrating a big milestone. Their financial plan had removed their financial fears and provided them with confidence of what they could do.

To me, that's living your life. It's empowering to know that you have the finances in place to do what you want to do. That you can live in the moment, enjoy life, and not worry about the future.

That's living in the Retirement Zone.

How to tell if you're in the zone

I opened our first chapter with a story about Michael Jordan enjoying a night against the Portland Trail Blazers in 1992 during which he nailed one three-pointer after another. It was easy to tell from that national telecast that Jordan, even by his lofty standards, was in the zone.

Most of us are not elite, professional athletes or performers. We aren't pouring in thirty-six points in a basketball game or playing a guitar solo from "Free Bird" that inspires the audience to light up their cellphones.

When it comes to financial security, the zone can be more subtle and harder to identify. Here, however, are five helpful signs that can help you determine if you have truly arrived in the Retirement Zone.

You feel empowered. You have the freedom to do what you want, when you want to do it. There's no reason to put things off because you're worried about time or resources.

You're confident. You have a plan that's working to fund your retirement. You not only feel secure in knowing that the money is there when you need it, but your actions demonstrate it.

You sleep well. Sure, you might not sleep as well as you did in your twenties, but you're not pacing the floor at 3 a.m., worrying about your finances or how your surviving spouse will manage after you pass away.

You're in the flow of life. Some people live in the past. Others are dreamers who dwell on the future. You're right in the middle, living each moment and not too concerned about what happened before, or what's coming next.

Examples of this might be spontaneous moments that embody the best version of you.

You do what you love to do. This is the essence of the Retirement Zone: you live out the vision you had for the ideal retirement and your perfect days, whatever that may mean to you.

Exceeding expectations

Sometimes, living in the Retirement Zone means realizing an even better life than you thought possible. Life after you retire might just be even better than you had imagined.

I'm reminded of a client couple whose dream was to spend more time with their grandchildren. However, this couple was still working, and they lived quite a distance from their children. It seemed that their future would involve continuing to work for many years, and only seeing the grandkids on infrequent trips and special occasions. This was but a dream to them, not even in their realm of possibilities to sell their house, retire and move. They didn't believe that was even an option.

But it was possible. In working together to build a solid, realistic financial plan, the couple was able to ask that question, "What if this could be true?" "What if we were able to spend more time with our grandchildren?" Remember those five questions from James Ryan in Chapter 4?

We built a plan around that idea and my clients realized that it was not only possible, but they could do it right now. Not because they had so much money, but because they had enough money. So, they sold their house, retired, and moved to the city where their children lived. And they get to spend more time with their grandkids than they could have ever imagined would be possible.

The security of a good financial plan empowered this couple to realize a retirement they thought was too good to be true. For me personally, it was gratifying to play a part in their goal, and to see the excited looks on their faces when they realized they could put their plan into action.

That is what's special to me about my job — that planning for retirement allows my clients to almost be a kid and dream again. Part of the financial planning process is to imagine how life could be, to take off those blinders you wore throughout your adulthood and say, "what is possible?"

Are you ready to enter the zone?

We've covered a lot of ground in this book, and we've only scratched the surface of some of the complexities of retirement planning.

Regardless of what you decide to do next in planning for retirement, I hope the one thing that you take away from this book is that this process really begins with you, and what you want the next several decades of your life to be like — starting today. A financial advisor can help you on this journey, but success really depends on your ability to articulate and envision your own personal Retirement Zone.

At LifePlan, our mission is to help our clients live the life they most wish to live, sooner rather than later. Helping to provide that fulfillment with life is our passion, and it's what gives us joy.

What are you passionate about? If you haven't already, write it down, and begin your journey to a new, fulfilling stage in life.

ABOUT THE AUTHOR

Alex has a mechanical engineering and trumpet performance degree from Iowa State University and a Masters in Business Administration (MBA) specializing in financial planning from California Lutheran University. Prior to joining LifePlan Group in 2012, he served as a public high school math teacher in Warren County, North

Carolina, through a program called Teach For America. After teaching algebra and pre-calculus, he worked as a math coach, mentoring other math teachers in North Carolina.

Alex is securities licensed as an investment advisor, where he serves as a fiduciary to his clients, working in their best interest. He is also life insurance, Medicare Supplement, and long-term care insurance licensed, real estate licensed, is a member of the Financial Planning Association and is a CERTIFIED FINANCIAL PLANNER™ Professional. Alex is a co-owner of LifePlan Group, along with his father, Ken Sutherland, and runs the day-to-day operations to best serve clients and prospective clients.

Outside of helping his clients live in the Retirement Zone, you'll find Alex chasing his three kids, Nora, Shea, and Elliot around the house, playing trumpet in his music studio, and enjoying a glass of wine with his wife, Lauren, post kid's bedtime!

Made in the USA
Columbia, SC
26 March 2025